Current Affairs

INGLÊS PRÁTICO: vestibulares e concursos

DANIEL VASCONCELOS | MARK G. NASH

Current Affairs

INGLÊS PRÁTICO: vestibulares e concursos

To Julia, Eric and Helena, as always.
Mark

À minha mãe, Marlene Vasconcelos (in memoriam),
que sempre acreditou em mim.
Daniel

© 2011 Daniel Vasconcelos e Mark Guy Nash

Preparação de texto
Juliane Kaori / Verba Editorial

Capa e projeto gráfico
Paula Astiz

Editoração eletrônica
Laura Lotufo / Paula Astiz Design

Assistente editorial
Aline Naomi Sassaki

Dados Internacionais de Catalogação na Publicação (CIP)
(Câmara Brasileira do Livro, SP, Brasil)

Vasconcelos, Daniel
  Current affairs : inglês prático para vestibulares e concursos / Daniel Vasconcelos, Mark G. Nash. – Barueri, SP : DISAL, 2011.

  ISBN 978-85-7844-076-3

  1. Inglês (Vestibular) 2. Inglês - Concursos 3. Inglês - Estudo e ensino I. Nash, Mark G.. II. Título.

11-05458   CDD-420.7

Índices para catálogo sistemático:
1. Inglês: Estudo e ensino   420.7

Todos os direitos reservados em nome de:
Bantim, Canato e Guazzelli Editora Ltda.

Alameda Mamoré 911 – cj. 107
Alphaville – BARUERI – SP
CEP: 06454-040
Tel. / Fax: (11) 4195-2811

Visite nosso site: www.disaleditora.com.br
Televendas: (11) 3226-3111
Fax gratuito: 0800 7707 105/106
E-mail para pedidos: comercialdisal@disal.com.br

Nenhuma parte desta publicação pode ser reproduzida, arquivada ou transmitida de nenhuma forma ou meio sem permissão expressa e por escrito da Editora.

	Introdução	9
1	Política Internacional no Mundo Pós-Guerra Fria	15
2	A Desvalorização do dólar norte-americano	21
3	Um Princípio Orientador para a Política Externa	27
4	A Usina Hidrelétrica de Belo Monte	33
5	A Eleição Presidencial de 2010	39
6	A "Guerra Cambial" entre os Estados Unidos e a China	47
7	A Declaração Diplomática Brasileira Contra Sanções ao Irã	53
8	Direitos de Propriedade e Subdesenvolvimento	57
9	Haiti: Instituições e Desenvolvimento	69
10	A Economia dos Impérios	73
11	A Política de Repressão aos Entorpecentes	79
12	WikiLeaks	83
13	A Revolução do Jasmim na Tunísia	89
14	Malária e Boa Governança	95
15	Julian Assange e seus Críticos Liberais	99
	Glossário dos termos mais importantes nos artigos	105
	Glossário de marcadores de discurso	121
	Respostas dos exercícios	131
	Sobre os autores	135

Introdução

1 Inglês e concursos públicos

O inglês é a língua das atualidades. Língua oficial em cerca de 70 países que representam conjuntamente cerca de 40% do PIB mundial, o inglês é a segunda maior língua nativa do mundo, depois do mandarim. Devido à influência desses países, o idioma tornou-se fundamental na diplomacia, no comércio internacional, na academia e no mundo científico. Estima-se que 85% das publicações científicas, 75% da comunicação internacional por escrito, 80% da informação armazenada nos computadores do mundo e até 90% do conteúdo da Internet são em inglês. Se considerarmos todas as pessoas que falam inglês como segunda língua, temos que reconhecê-la como a língua mais falada no planeta. Em qualquer canto do mundo, os negócios internacionais são conduzidos em inglês, tornando-a a língua franca do mundo. No Brasil isso não poderia ser diferente. Domínio do inglês é exigido no mercado de trabalho e na educação.

Concursos públicos são, hoje em dia, muito competitivos. Milhões de brasileiros almejam um emprego no Estado, principalmente porque os salários são, em média, muito superiores àqueles praticados na iniciativa privada. Em recente pesquisa elaborada pelo Dieese (Departamento Intersindical de Estatística e Estudos Socioeconômicos) confirmou-se que os servidores públicos ganham em média 98% a mais que funcionários da iniciativa privada. Por isso mesmo, grande parte das pessoas mais capacitadas no Brasil direciona-se ao setor público. Diante da acirrada disputa pelas vagas disponíveis, um número significativo de pessoas dedica-se exclusivamente ao estudo para os concursos públicos.

Todos os anos, milhões de brasileiros prestam concursos, seja para estudar em universidades públicas, trabalhar em empresas estatais ou no governo. A maioria das provas tem um componente importante de avaliação de língua inglesa. Se você é um desses milhões de brasileiros se preparando para fazer um concurso público, este livro é para você.

Preparando para concuros e vestibulares

Uma das principais dificuldades na preparação para concursos públicos está em encontrar material de qualidade especificamente voltado para preparar os estudantes e profissionais para as provas de concursos. Geralmente, pode-se adquirir cópias das provas de anos anteriores, muito útil na análise da natureza e da lógica dos exames, mas infelizmente com conteúdo desatualizado. Os textos utilizados em exames públicos, inevitavelmente, envolvem assuntos atuais de interesse estratégico para o Brasil e região. Tentaremos corrigir essa falta de material para preparar o candidato para as provas de língua inglesa nos concursos nas páginas a seguir.

Este livro contém 15 artigos originais extraídos de jornais e fontes de mídia de países de língua inglesa. Os temas abordados nos artigos são alguns dos mais importantes da atualidade e refletem os temas que aparecerão em concursos públicos em futuro próximo. Cada artigo tem um glossário bilíngue que explora as colocações, expressões, termos e neologismos usados no discurso jornalístico para discutir atualidades. Os glossários são muito úteis para apreender e consolidar a linguagem necessária para ler e compreender artigos de jornais e revistas em inglês.

Cada artigo tem uma breve introdução para contextualizar o autor e o assunto. Após o artigo há perguntas nos moldes dos concursos públicos. As questões oferecem uma excelente oportunidade para avaliar a compreensão do texto, além de fornecer exemplos claros dos tipos de questões encontrados em provas de inglês nos concursos. Esses textos e questões proporcionam uma excelente forma de preparação para os próximos vestibulares e concursos públicos.

No final do livro incluímos um apêndice, em ordem alfabética, das colocações, expressões e termos mais importantes dos artigos. O leitor deste livro deve conhecer este vocabulário, que certamente aparecerá em outros textos de concursos. Incluímos também um segundo glossário de "marcadores de discurso", ou seja, palavras e expressões altamente convencionais que são usadas para organizar o discurso. O glossário ajudará o leitor a compreender a organização de textos e da linguagem utilizada para a "sinalização" no gênero jornalístico.

Quem deve se beneficiar deste livro

Concurseiros e vestibulandos. Alunos preparando-se para vestibulares e, principalmente, pessoas preparando-se para um concurso público vão beneficiar-se muito com este livro.

Professores e alunos de inglês. O ensino de línguas tem evoluído muito nos últimos anos com a nova abordagem lexical baseada em "pedaços de linguagem" (*chunks of language*). Essa abordagem tem se mostrado muito mais eficaz do que o ensino convencional baseado na gramática e na memorização de vocábulos individuais. Essa mudança surgiu a partir do reconhecimento de que a linguagem humana é fundamentalmente baseada em conjuntos de palavras, ou *chunks* (pedaços), que aparecem com grande frequência, na forma de colocações, expressões, frases fixas e semifixas. Neste livro, adotamos a abordagem lexical na análise de textos originais e altamente relevantes no mundo de hoje.

Os textos selecionados serão úteis para professores e alunos de inglês por serem textos autênticos que exploram a linguagem das atualidades no gênero jornalístico. Os glossários bilíngues e as perguntas ajudarão a explorar a matéria com grande eficiência. Os textos também abordam muitos dos "temas transversais" enfocados nos Parâmetros Curriculares Nacionais — PCNs — referências para o ensino de todo o País.

2 Como se preparar para um concurso

Estratégias de prova para concursos públicos: orientações gerais

- Não subestime a prova. Todas as provas são difíceis e exigem conhecimento especializado.
- Estude o edital, os guias de estudo e as provas anteriores. É importante focar somente nas matérias que vão cair na prova.
- Não fique obcecado pela remuneração. Procure adequar o seu perfil ao estilo do cargo.
- Não pense em um só concurso. Participe de todos que você achar interessante, mesmo se for um pouco fora da sua área. Cada prova serve como treino para futuros concursos.
- Conheça as peculiaridades e a "lógica" da banca examinadora.
- Apenas fazer cursinho não é o suficiente. Estabeleça uma rotina diária de estudos.
- Os colegas de classe não são inimigos. A mentalidade de "soma zero", infelizmente, é muito comum. Procure aliar-se a outras pessoas que estão na mesma situação.
- Não pense no total de concorrentes. Muitos deles não estão preparados e assim não são verdadeiros concorrentes.
- Reconheça que estudar para concurso público é um projeto de longo prazo. Em muitos casos, será necessária uma dedicação de vários anos para assimilar as matérias.
- Lembre-se que a prova é documento oficial e, portanto, não pode contradizer uma posição oficial do Estado.
- Organize bem o seu tempo de estudo. Não se esqueça de programar horas de descanso, atividade física e lazer para evitar que você fique esgotado.

Orientações para as provas de língua inglesa

- Geralmente, as provas de língua inglesa consistem em pequenos textos seguidos por algumas questões.
- As questões geralmente seguem a mesma ordem de apresentação das ideias no texto.

- As questões muitas vezes consistem em múltiplas partes a serem julgadas individualmente como certo ou errado (C ou E).
- Há também questões de múltipla escolha nas quais o candidato precisa selecionar uma resposta correta ou incorreta, dependendo do comando da questão.
- Preste atenção à pontuação da prova. Nas provas do Cespe (Centro de Seleção e de Promoção de Eventos), por exemplo, as questões do tipo "certo ou errado" (C ou E) valem um quarto de ponto quando marcadas corretamente. Em contrapartida, subtrai-se um quarto de ponto quando marcadas incorretamente. Questões de múltipla escolha valem 1 ponto quando marcadas corretamente mas só perdem 0,20 ponto se marcadas incorretamente. Concentre-se nestas questões.
- As publicações mais usadas nos concursos são: *The Economist, The New York Times, Newsweek, BusinessWeek* e *The Wall Street Journal*. Procure ler essas publicações.

Tipos de questões

Há três tipos de questões nas provas:
a) Questões que cobram informações específicas do texto.
b) Questões interpretativas que buscam aferir o conhecimento da língua.
c) Questões interpretativas que aferem a capacidade de compreender a mensagem e o propósito do texto.

Estratégias específicas

a) Cada banca estrutura a prova de forma diferente, portanto é imprescindível ler as instruções na página inicial e os comandos das questões com cuidado. Procure provas anteriores e familiarize-se antecipadamente com o formato.
b) Ao abordar o texto, leia o título e a fonte no final do texto para ter uma ideia geral do que se trata. A fonte o ajudará a contextualizá-lo.
c) Nas provas de inglês, sempre leia as questões antes do texto. Isso ajuda a focar a leitura para resolver as questões e poupa tempo.
d) Sublinhe no comando da questão as palavras-chave, especialmente se houver uma negação (exemplos: "select which is not correct" ou "all are correct except").
e) Na primeira leitura do texto, identifique e sublinhe as palavras-chave que possam ajudar a resolver as questões.
f) Procure eliminar as respostas "absurdas" e concentre-se nas plausíveis.
g) Para o examinador, desde que a afirmação não seja estritamente falsa, ela está correta. (parece óbvio, mas não é). Em outras palavras, a resposta pode estar incompleta, mas do ponto de vista lógico não está errada. Infelizmente, isso depende da banca examinadora. Exemplo: um texto hipotético contém oito verbos. Mas a questão afirma que há quatro verbos no texto. Na banca do Cespe, por exemplo, esta afirmação seria considerada correta, já que há (estrita-

mente falando) quatro verbos no parágrafo. Seria errada se fosse escrito: há somente 4 verbos no texto.

h) Algumas vezes, não há uma opção perfeita. Escolha a melhor possível, a mais correta.

1

Política internacional no mundo pós-Guerra Fria

Em seu provocativo ensaio intitulado "O choque das civilizações", o cientista político Samuel Huntington defendeu a tese de que cultura e religião tornar-se-iam as principais fontes de conflito geopolítico no mundo pós-Guerra Fria. Huntington, professor na Universidade de Harvard, foi membro do Conselho de Segurança Nacional dos Estados Unidos durante a administração Carter. Seu ensaio, publicado na revista Foreign Affairs em 1993, insere-se num contexto de grande efervescência nos debates sobre a "ordem mundial" pós-Guerra Fria. No artigo a seguir, Dominique Moisi, fundador do Instituto Francês de Relações Internacionais, oferece uma reavaliação da perspectiva huntingtoniana e sugere que os conflitos internacionais não são realmente embates civilizacionais, mas podem, simplesmente, ser explicados pelos sentimentos de subjugação de certas populações.

The clash of civilisations is really one of emotions

1 Throughout the **"war on terror"**, the notion of a **"clash of civilisations"** between Islam and **the West** has usually been dismissed as **politically incorrect** and **intellectually wrongheaded**. **Instead**, the most
5 common interpretation has been that the world **has entered a new era** characterised by conflict "within" a particular civilisation, **namely** Islam, with **fundamentalist Muslims** as much at war against moderates from within their own religious
10 community as against the West.
    The strategic conclusion derived from such an analysis was clear, ambitious, and easily summarised: democratisation. If the absence of democracy in the Islamic world was the problem,
15 then bringing democracy to **the Greater Middle**

war on terror: expressão norte-americana relacionada principalmente às ações militares daquele Estado em vários países, como no Iraque e no Afeganistão

clash of civilisations: o choque de civilizações é uma teoria proposta pelo cientista político Samuel Huntington segundo a qual as identidades culturais e religiosas dos povos tornar-se-iam a principal fonte de conflito no mundo pós-Guerra Fria

the West: o Ocidente

politically incorrect: politicamente incorreto

intellectually wrongheaded: intelectualmente equivocado

instead: (marcador de discurso que introduz um contraste) pelo contrário, por outro lado

East would be the solution, and it was the historical duty of the United States, as the most powerful and moral nation, **to bring about** that necessary change. **The status quo was untenable**. Implementing democracy, with or without **regime change**, was the only alternative to chaos and **the rise of fundamentalism**.

Today, Iraq may be **on the verge of civil war** between Shiites and Sunnis. Iran under a new and more radical president is **moving irresistibly towards** possessing a nuclear capacity. A **free electoral process brought Hamas to power** in Palestine, and the **unfortunate episode** of the Danish newspaper cartoons illustrated the **almost combustible nature of relations** between Islam and the West.

All of these developments are **paving the way** to new interpretations. **Rather than** a "clash of civilisations", we might instead be faced by **multiple layers of conflict**, which interact with each other in ways that increase global instability.

Indeed, it appears that the world is witnessing a triple conflict. There is **a clash within Islam** which, if the violence in Iraq **spreads** to neighbouring countries, risks causing regional destabilisation. There is also a clash that is best described not as being between Islam and the West, but between the secularised world and a growing religious one. At an even deeper and atavistic level, there is an emotional clash between a culture of fear and a culture of humiliation.

It would be a **gross oversimplification** to speak, as some are doing, of a **clash between civilisation and barbarism**. In reality, we are **confronted with a widening divide** over the role of religion, which runs between the West (with the United States being a complicated exception) and **much of the rest of the world** (the most notable exception being China), but particularly the Islamic world.

The divide reflects how religion defines an individual's identity within a society. At a time when religion is becoming **increasingly important**

---

has entered a new era: começou uma nova era
namely: referindo-se em particular a, ou seja
fundamentalist Muslims: muçulmanos fundamentalistas
the Greater Middle East: neologismo da administração Bush para se referir a um grupo de países islâmicos além do Oriente Médio, e que inclui a Turquia, Irã, Afeganistão e Paquistão
to bring about: fazer acontecer
the status quo was untenable: as condições vigentes estavam insustentáveis
regime change: expressão usada nos Estados Unidos desde 1925 para se referir à mudança de governos e instituições em outros países. Tornou-se amplamente usada nos governos Clinton e Bush para definir a política norte-americana em relação ao Estado iraquiano.
the rise of fundamentalism: a ascendência do fundamentalismo
on the verge of civil war: à beira de uma guerra civil
moving irresistibly towards: ir em direção a algo ou algum objetivo sem hesitação
free electoral process: processo eleitoral livre e democrático
brought Hamas to power: levou o Hamas ao poder
unfortunate episode: acontecimento lamentável
almost combustible nature of relations: uma relação tensa e potencialmente explosiva que pode tornar-se conflituosa a qualquer momento
paving the way: facilitando, abrindo caminho
rather than: (marcador de discurso que introduz uma alternativa) ao invés de
multiple layers of conflict: conflitos complexos que não podem ser reduzidos a apenas uma causa
indeed: (marcador de discurso para enfatizar antes de afirmar algo) de fato
a clash within Islam: um conflito interno no Islã
spreads: se alastra

elsewhere, we Europeans **have largely forgotten our (violent and intolerant) religious past**, and we have difficulty understanding **the role that religion can play** in other peoples' daily lives.

In some ways, "they" are our own **buried past** and, with a combination of ignorance, prejudice and, **above all**, fear, "we" are afraid that "they" could define our future. We live in a secular world, where **free speech** can **easily turn into** insensitive and irresponsible **mockery**, while others see religion as their **supreme goal**, if not their **last hope**. They have tried everything, from nationalism to regionalism, from communism to capitalism. Since everything has failed, why not **give God a chance**?

Globalisation may not have created these layers of conflicts, but it has accelerated them by making the differences more visible and palpable. In our globalised age, we have lost the privilege — and, paradoxically, the virtue — of ignorance. We all see how others feel and react, but without the minimal **historical and cultural tools necessary to decipher those reactions**. Globalisation has paved the way to a world **dominated by the dictatorship of emotions** — and of ignorance.

This clash of emotions is exacerbated in the case of Islam. In the Arab world, in particular, Islam is dominated by a culture of humiliation felt by the people and nations that consider themselves **the main losers**, the worst victims, of a new and unjust international system. **From that standpoint**, the Israel-Palestine conflict is exemplary. It has become an obsession.

It is not so much that Arabs and Muslims really care about the Palestinians. **On the contrary**, the Islamic world left the Palestinians without real support for decades. In reality, for them the conflict **has come to symbolise** the anachronistic perpetuation of an **unfair colonial order**, to represent their **political malaise**, and to embody the perceived impossibility of their being **masters of their destiny**.

In the eyes of the Arabs (and some other

---

gross oversimplification: simplificação exagerada

clash between civilization and barbarism: conflito entre a civilização e a barbárie

confronted with a widening divide: deparando-se com uma crescente divisão

much of the rest of the world: grande parte do resto do mundo

increasingly important: cada vez mais importante

have largely forgotten our (violent and intolerant) religious past: quase nos esquecemos totalmente de nosso passado religioso (violento e intolerante)

the role that religion can play: o papel que pode ser desempenhado pela religião

buried past: passado esquecido (literalmente, enterrado)

above all: acima de tudo

free speech: liberdade de expressão

easily turn into: facilmente pode tornar-se

mockery: gozação ou zombaria

supreme goal: o objetivo principal

last hope: última esperança

give God a chance: dê uma chance a Deus

historical and cultural tools necessary to decipher those reactions: as ferramentas (mentais) históricas e culturais necessárias para decifrar aquelas reações

dominated by the dictatorship of emotions: expressão usada pelo autor para transmitir a ideia de que o discurso no mundo globalizado é dominado por emoções exacerbadas

the main losers: os mais prejudicados

from that standpoint: a partir desse ponto de vista

it is not so much that: não se pode dizer realmente que

on the contrary: (marcador de discurso que apresenta um oposição) pelo contrário

has to come to symbolise: tornou-se simbólico

unfair colonial order: estrutura colonial injusta

Muslims), Israel's strength and resilience is a direct consequence of their own weakness, divisions and corruption. The majority of Arabs may not support Al-Qaeda, but they do not oppose it **with all their heart**. Instead, there is the temptation to regard Osama bin Laden as a violent Robin Hood, whose actions, while impossible to condone officially, have helped **to regain a sense of Arab pride** and dignity.

Here, perhaps, is the real clash of civilisations: the emotional conflict between the European culture of fear and the Muslim, particularly Arab, culture of humiliation. It would be dangerous to underestimate **the depth of so wide an emotional divide**; recognising its existence is **the first step toward overcoming it**. But that will be difficult, for **transcending the emotional clash of civilisations** presupposes an opening to the "other" that neither side may yet be ready to undertake.

DOMINIQUE MOISI
www.dailystar.com.lb

political malaise: mal-estar político
masters of their destiny: donos de seu próprio destino
in the eyes of the Arabs: do ponto de vista dos árabes
with all their heart: de forma veemente, de coração
to regain a sense of Arab pride: reconquistar o orgulho árabe
the depth of so wide an emotional divide: a severidade de uma divisão emocional tão grande
the first step toward overcoming it: o primeiro passo para superá-lo
transcending the emotional clash of civilisations: ir além do conflito emocional entre as civilizações

Nota sobre ortografia: esse artigo foi escrito usando a ortografia britânica, com "s" e não "z" nas palavras "civilisation", "globalisation", "democratisation" e "destabilisation", e com "u" em "neighbouring".

A palavra civilização vem do latim *civilis*, que significa civil, cortês, polido. O termo é também relacionado a *civis*, cidadão, e *civitas*, cidade. Civilização é um termo controverso que tem sido usado para se referir a fenômenos distintos. Originalmente, a palavra foi usada para se referir a sociedades complexas em termos de tecnologia, política e divisão do trabalho. No contexto da história clássica, os povos que se consideravam civilizados se contrastavam aos povos "bárbaros" (aqueles que não falavam grego). Nas discussões acadêmicas modernas, há uma tendência de usar o termo de uma forma mais neutra, no sentido de "cultura". Usa-se a palavra, também, no sentido de refinamento ou alta elaboração cultural.

Questions

1 **The reference to the "episode in the Danish newspaper" (line 28) refers to:**
   a) the publication of cartoon drawings considered offensive to Muslims
   b) racist commentaries by Danish editors

c) the prohibition of material published in that country
   d) the closure of the newspaper due to international pressure
   e) the publication of American war secrets

2 **The phrase "almost combustible nature of relations" (line 29) refers to:**
   a) a situation that can quickly be used up
   b) a tense situation where there is a lack of combustible fuel
   c) a situation without major tensions where peace prevails
   d) a relationship that can't be terminated
   e) a tense situation that is always close to becoming violent

3 **The author argues that calling the conflict between Islam and the West a "clash of civilizations":**
   a) is motivated by purely economic forces
   b) is an oversimplification of the complex conflict between Islam and the West
   c) refers to the clash within Islam between fundamentalist Muslims and moderates
   d) helps to alleviate misunderstanding between Islam and the West

4 **The term "gross oversimplification" (line 47) can best be translated as:**
   a) simplificação exagerada
   b) simplificação grosseira
   c) desrespeito
   d) simplificação temerária

5 **In the sentence below, the author uses "they" and "we" to refer to, respectively:**

   In some ways, "they" are our own buried past and, with a combination of ignorance, prejudice and, above all, fear, "we" are afraid that "they" could define our future.

   a) Europeans and Muslims
   b) Muslims and Americans
   c) Muslims and Europeans
   d) Europeans and Americans
   e) Americans and Muslims

6 **The modal verb "may" in the sentence "Globalisation may not have created these layers of conflicts" (line 72) expresses:**
   a) probability
   b) causality

c) obligation
d) possibility
e) certainty

7 **Judge the following item.**

In the sentence below, "them" refers to "globalisation". (C) (E)

*Globalisation may not have created these layers of conflicts, but it has accelerated **them** by making the differences more visible and palpable.*

8 **The word "resilience" (line 100) could be correctly replaced by:**
a) steadfastness
b) resourcefulness
c) consistence
d) weakness
e) patience

9 **In the sentence below, "with all their heart" could be correctly replaced with "wholeheartedly".** (C) (E)

*The majority of Arabs may not support Al-Qaeda, but they do not oppose it **with all their heart**.*

10 **On line 113 the author states that the first step to overcoming what he calls an "emotional clash of civilizations" is:**
a) to underestimate the gap between such a wide emotional divide
b) to recognize the other is wrong
c) to presuppose your own superiority
d) to seek ways to secularize the Middle East
e) to recognize the widespread feelings of fear or humiliation experienced by individuals from different nations

11 **The new perception regarding international conflicts advocated in the text involves:**
a) realizing that Muslims feel victimized
b) recognizing that feelings and emotions play a key role in international conflict
c) recognizing the insolubility of international conflict
d) recognizing that they are essentially clashes between civilizations
e) recognizing that the West is more civilized

2

A desvalorização do dólar norte-americano

O dólar norte-americano é a moeda mais importante para compor reservas e para efetuar transações internacionais. Em decorrência desse fato, a desvalorização do dólar, ao longo dos últimos anos, tem sido alvo de fortes críticas. Neste artigo, o deputado norte-americano Ron Paul oferece uma análise sóbria sobre a política inflacionária de seu governo e as consequências dessa política para os cidadãos comuns.

More inflation fears

Inflation fears are heating up this week as **Fed Chairman** Ben Bernanke gave a speech in Boston on Friday, causing further **frantic flight into gold** by those fearful of the coming **"quantitative easing"** the Fed is set to deliver in November. Others who view gold as a **short-term investment** engaged in immediate **profit-taking** after Bernanke's speech.

Gold is more correctly viewed as **insurance against bad monetary policy decisions** that **erode the value of savings**. Those bad decisions keep coming at **an ever faster clip** these days and we hear more and more talk of **currency wars** especially between the dollar, the Chinese yuan, the Japanese yen, the Australian dollar, and the Euro. As the economies of the world continue to **stagnate** or **contract**, monetary policy decisions become more relevant to people who once thought this topic **arcane**. We have several examples this week of **major fumbles** on the part of the US Central Bank:

1) The Federal Reserve **continues to insist** that

inflation fears are heating up: o medo da inflação está se exacerbando
Fed Chairman: diretor do banco central norte-americano
frantic flight into gold: compra "frenética" de ouro motivada pelo medo da perda do valor da moeda norte-americana
quantitative easing: "relaxamento quantitativo", refere-se a uma política monetária que visa aumentar a quantidade de dinheiro
the Fed: forma abreviada do nome do banco central norte-americano (Federal Reserve), sempre usado com o artigo "the"
short-term investment: investimento de curto prazo
profit-taking: realização de lucros
insurance against bad monetary policy decisions: um "hedge" (proteção cambial) ou uma proteção contra decisões prejudiciais de política monetária
erode the value of savings: acarretam a perda de valor real de uma poupança

inflation is too low, even while the **monetary base** remains at record levels, and **food and gas prices continue to climb.**

2) As the Fed continues to **drive down the value of the dollar**, the government accuses China of **deliberately devaluing its currency**, and **the House has passed legislation aimed at punishing China for this alleged devaluation**.

3) **Low returns on US bonds** are **driving investors into higher-performing foreign bonds**. Some of these countries are responding by reinstituting **capital controls** to guard against **hot money** and the **carry trade**.

4) The **spat** with China and reemergence of capital controls have led some to fear that we are in the first stages of an **all-out** currency war.

5) The instability in the **international monetary system**, the decreasing value of the dollar, and the large amounts of new **US debt** could lead the **IMF** and countries such as China, Japan, Russia, India, and Brazil to abandon the dollar and adopt a new multinational currency.

While the big players in these currency games sort everything out, the people hurt the most are the **savers**, the workers, and **those on fixed incomes** as their money buys less and less. **Make no mistake** — the Fed and the **Treasury Department** are playing games with our money, especially in how they report statistics like unemployment and inflation. These games **erode our standard of living** and hide just how much damage their **inflationary policies** are doing.

Official **core inflation** for the US is only 1.14%, but that excludes such crucial **day-to-day goods** as food and energy. **Real inflation** certainly is higher, maybe much higher. John Williams of *Shadow Government Statistics* calculates **true inflation**

---

an even faster clip: em velocidade cada vez maior
currency wars: "guerra de moedas", uma desvalorização competitiva entre países
stagnate: estagnar
contract: encolher, contrair
arcane: misterioso, obscuro
major fumbles: grandes erros, grandes besteiras
continues to insist: continua a afirmar, insistir
monetary base: a base monetária, ou seja, a quantidade total de dinheiro impresso pelo governo
food and gas prices continue to climb: o preço de alimentos e de gasolina continuam subindo
drive down the value of the dollar: reduzir o valor do dólar
deliberately devaluing its currency: desvalorizar intencionalmente a sua moeda
the House: a Câmara dos Deputados
has passed legislation aimed at punishing China for this alleged devaluation: aprovou uma lei que almeja punir a China por sua alegada desvalorização
low returns on US bonds: baixos retornos nos títulos do governo norte-americano
driving investors into higher-performing foreign bonds: levando investidores a procurar títulos estrangeiros mais rentáveis
capital controls: controle de capitais
hot money: capitais especulativos
carry trade: prática de pegar dinheiro emprestado em um país com juros baixos e aplicá-lo em um país com juros altos
spat: briga, conflito
all-out: sem restrições, sem limites
international monetary system: o sistema monetário internacional
US debt: a dívida do governo norte-americano
IMF: Fundo Monetário Internacional (FMI)
while the big players in these currency games sort everything out: enquanto os atores dominantes nesse "jogo de moedas" resolvem as coisas
savers: poupadores, as pessoas que pouparam dinheiro ao longo da vida

at a **whopping** 8.48%! But manipulated inflation statistics **give the government cover** when they again deny seniors a **cost-of-living increase** in their **social security checks**. They also serve to convince the public that further **expansion of the money supply** will **boost the economy** without causing any real pain, which has essentially been the **core argument** of Greenspan-Bernanke fed policy for the last 20 years.

Of course, the United States is not alone in its disastrous monetary policy decisions. These pressures are inherent in any **fiat monetary system** where money is **created at will**, for the benefit of the **special interests**. As all these currencies **race to the bottom of the inflationary barrel**, the only security to be had will be in honest money like gold as the system **falls apart**. My hope is that we can return to the wisdom of the Constitution and get back to **sound, commodity-backed money** before our dollar suffers a **wholesale collapse.**

Ron Paul – October 26, 2010
http://www.ronpaularchive.com/

---

those on fixed incomes: aqueles que vivem de aposentadorias, pensões e outras fontes de renda fixa
make no mistake: não se iluda
Treasury Department: instituição governamental norte-americana que emite moeda e títulos
erode our standard of living: prejudicam a qualidade de vida
inflationary policies: políticas inflacionárias
core inflation: uma das estatísticas usadas para medir o aumento do nível de preços no "cerne" da economia, que não leva em consideração alimentos ou energia
day-to-day goods: bens de consumo básicos, como alimentos e combustível
real inflation: inflação real
true inflation: inflação verdadeira
whopping: incrível, surpreendente
give the government cover: dão cobertura ao governo, justificam suas ações
cost-of-living increase: reajuste de acordo com o aumento do nível de preços
social security checks: pagamento de aposentadorias
expansion of the money supply: aumento da quantidade de dinheiro
boost the economy: estimular a economia
core argument: argumento central
of course: (marcador de discurso para enfatizar), claro, certamente, com certeza, claramente
fiat monetary system: sistema monetário no qual a moeda nacional não tem lastro ou conversibilidade em ouro, outro metal ou commodity
created at will: criado arbitrariamente
special interests: interesses políticos
race to the bottom of the inflationary barrel: mergulham para o fundo do poço inflacionário
falls apart: se desmorona
sound, commodity-backed money: moeda forte com garantia de conversibilidade em alguma commodity (matérias-primas) como ouro
wholesale collapse: um colapso generalizado

O "dollar" é o nome da moeda em 14 países, incluindo o Canadá, Hong Kong, Austrália, Nova Zelândia e Estados Unidos. A palavra "dollar" vem de uma moeda de prata produzida no século XVI na República Tcheca, chamada *Joachimsthaler*, ou simplesmente *thaler*. O dólar norte-americano é a moeda oficial dos Estados Unidos da América, Equador, El Salvador e Panamá. Há, também, muitos países que atrelam o valor de suas moedas ao dólar. A mais significativa dessas moedas atreladas é o renminbi (iuan) chinês.

Questions

1. When the author says "inflation fears are heating up" he means inflation fears are:
   a) causing people to become angry
   b) decreasing in intensity
   c) increasing in intensity
   d) becoming unreasonable

2. According to the author, Ron Paul, the "flight into gold" is motivated by:
   a) a fear of holding US dollars that are losing and will continue to lose their value
   b) a fear of deflation
   c) a fear of Chinese retaliation against US measures to devalue the dollar
   d) low interest rates in the US
   e) capital flowing to developing economies

3. The actions of the US government in the week prior to the writing of the article are seen by the author as:
   a) a necessary measure to fight inflation
   b) a good decision
   c) inevitable, given the stagnant US economy
   d) a big mistake
   e) a retaliation against China

4. The declining value of the US dollar can be attributed to:
   a) the declining value of the Chinese yuan
   b) the "flight into gold"
   c) inflation
   d) the rise of commodity prices
   e) deliberate efforts on behalf of the Fed to reduce its value

5 In the sentence "Low returns on US bonds are *driving* investors into higher-performing foreign bonds", the word "driving" can be correctly replaced with:
   a) sending
   b) calling
   c) transporting
   d) provoking
   e) influencing

6 According to the article, international fears of more "quantitative easing" and US dollar instability could result in:
   a) the use of the yuan as an international trade currency
   b) the abandoning of the US dollar as the common trade currency among nations like Brazil, China, Russia, Japan and India
   c) the massive selling of gold to preserve the dollar
   d) the buying of US dollar bonds on the international market

7 The author, Congressman Ron Paul, believes the actions of the US government will:
   a) lead to lower prices for basic goods for US citizens and erode their savings
   b) lead to higher prices of basic goods for US citizens and erode their savings
   c) lead to higher prices for basic goods for US citizens because of the devalued Chinese yuan
   d) increase most US citizen's savings because of the lower value of the US dollar

8 With regard to "official core inflation", the author believes that:
   a) it reflects the level of inflation that Americans really experience
   b) it is currently at 8.48%
   c) the US government is honest and transparent in reporting inflation
   d) it is not a good indicator of inflation because it doesn't include basic expenses like food and energy

9 According to the article, "quantitative easing" is likely to result in all except one of the following:
   a) the purchase of gold to preserve personal wealth
   b) inflation
   c) a decrease in the cost of living
   d) "currency wars" in which other nations will also attempt to devalue their currencies

10 Judge the following items:
   a) on line 50, the word "those" refers back to "people"   (C) (E)
   b) on line 68, "boost" means the same as "subsidize"   (C) (E)
   c) on line 82, "wholesale" could mean "generalized"   (C) (E)
   d) on line 65, "seniors" means the same as "the elderly"   (C) (E)

11 The purpose of the article is:
   a) to inform US citizens of the dangers of current US monetary policy
   b) to warn readers that the US dollar will lose even more of its value
   c) to suggest a return to a commodity-based dollar
   d) all of the above

3

Um princípio orientador para a política externa

Stephen Krasner é professor de relações internacionais na Universidade de Stanford. Neste artigo, o professor argumenta contra a elaboração de uma política exterior que visa grandes estratégias abrangentes, e a favor do estabelecimento de uma "soberania responsável".

An orienting principle for foreign policy

1 The deficiencies of "Grand Strategy"

Only **policy makers** in **great-power nations** can **aspire to** realize grand strategies. They rarely succeed. In the contemporary **international environment**, coherence is more likely to be achieved by **aiming at** something more modest, a principle around which foreign policy might be oriented. **Responsible sovereignty** is the most **promising candidate**. Responsible sovereignty focuses on the need to create states capable of governing effectively **within their own borders** and to realizing, where possible, **mutually beneficial bargains** with regard to global **public goods**. **Irresponsible sovereigns** and **failing states threaten the well-being of their own populations** and the security, **domestic norms**, and **authority structures** of even the world's most powerful countries. There is no alternative to responsible sovereigns; no regional much less global authority structure can replace the state.

The elusive Holy Grail

Grand strategy is a **conceptual framing** that

---

orienting principle: princípio que serve de guia, princípio orientador
foreign policy: política externa
grand strategy: estratégia abrangente, paradigma universal
policy makers: formuladores de políticas públicas
great-power nations: as grandes potências, nações dominantes no cenário internacional
aspire to: almejar, aspirar a
international environment: cenário internacional
aiming at: almejar
responsible sovereignty: soberania responsável
promising candidate: candidato promissor
within their own borders: internamente, dentro das fronteiras nacionais
mutually beneficial bargains: barganhas ou acordos mutuamente benéficos
public goods: bens públicos
irresponsible sovereigns: governos irresponsáveis
failing states: Estados fracassados
threaten the well-being of their

describes how the world is, envisions how it ought to be, and specifies a set of policies that can achieve that ordering. Grand strategies are designed to **mold the international environment** by **regulating international regimes**, influencing the foreign policy choices made by other states, and **shaping** or even determining the **domestic regime** characteristics of other countries. A successful grand strategy will have the support of some other major states. It will be **heuristically powerful**: able to **guide policy** across **a wide range of issue areas**. It will provide resources — diplomatic, bureaucratic, **ideational**, military, economic — for specific policies.

Most attempts at grand strategy fail: It is hard to **align** vision, policies, and resources. Some fail because they envision a world that cannot be realized. Others fail because resources cannot be aligned with policies because of **institutional constraints** or a lack of domestic or international political support.

Empirically, successful grand strategies have rarely started with a **clearly articulated vision** that was then implemented through **targeted policies** and associated resource allocations. The international environment with its multiple actors, conflicting interests, changing technological dynamics, and exposure to unexpected shocks is too complex for such a rational process. Rather, successful grand strategies are consolidated after a series of debates or **missteps** by linking polices and resources with an **overarching vision**.

Successful grand strategies are most likely when the two great defining variables of the international system — power and beliefs — **cleave along the same lines**. The clearest example of such a **cleavage** over the last two centuries was the division between the Soviet Union and the United States between 1945 and 1990, and the most successful grand strategy of the last two centuries was **containment**.

Bismarck's *Dreikaiserbund*, in contrast, was an impressive effort to solidify Germany's gains after

own populations: ameaçam o bem-estar de sua própria população
domestic norms: leis nacionais
authority structures: instituições governamentais
the elusive Holy Grail: o santo remédio elusivo (Holy Grail, o "Cálice Sagrado" usado na Última Ceia, refere-se a um objetivo quase impossível de ser realizado, mas que seria de grande benefício para a humanidade)
conceptual framing: arcabouço conceitual
mold the international environment: moldar o ambiente internacional
regulating international regimes: controlando governos no âmbito internacional
shaping: moldando, determinando
domestic regime: governo nacional
heuristically powerful: usando métodos eficazes para resolução de problemas
guide policy: balizar, guiar as políticas públicas
a wide range of issue areas: um amplo espectro de assuntos
ideational: relacionado às ideias
align: coordenar, alinhar
institutional constraints: limitações institucionais
clearly articulated vision: visão claramente articulada
targeted policies: políticas com alvo específico

missteps: erros
overarching vision: visão ou modelo abrangente

cleave along the same lines: alinham-se
cleavage: divisão

containment: a contenção foi uma política dos Estados Unidos durante a Guerra Fria que usava estratégias militares, econômicas e diplomáticas contra a propagação do comunismo no âmbito internacional

the Franco-Prussian War but ultimately **foundered** not just on the impulsiveness of Bismarck's successors but also on the fact that while ideology united Germany, Russia, and Austria-Hungary, power considerations divided them: Given Germany's power, France and Russia would **naturally be drawn to each other**.

A successful grand strategy then requires: an accurate understanding of the international environment; a vision of what that environment might become by: shaping international regimes, **altering the opportunity sets facing other states**, and influencing domestic authority structures in other states; a set of policies that can **realize that vision**; heuristic power to define policies for **unforeseen challenges**; an organizational structure within the state that can **implement these policies**; resources, and hence domestic **political support**, to pay for these policies; support from other actors in the international system who **share the same vision** and endorse the associated policies even if their material contributions are modest. Such support **is more likely** when power and ideology cleave along the same lines.

An alternative: orienting principles

Most foreign policies most of the time have not been guided by a grand strategy. The most obvious alternative to grand strategy is **no strategy at all**.

Policymakers attempt to maximize the two material interests of their states: economic and security. The environment — international regimes, the domestic authority structures of other states — is **taken as given**. Reliance on one or more orienting principles is a second alternative to grand strategy. Orienting principles provide a description of some elements of the existing environment and a vision for how they might be transformed.

A foreign policy based on an orienting principle differs from one motivated by a successful grand strategy in four ways. **First**, orienting principles **focus on** specific issue-areas. **Second**, there is no consensus, either domestically or internationally, about the extant situation or what it might become. **Third, there is ongoing uncertainty** about what policies might be most effective. **Fourth,** because of this uncertainty policies will not necessarily be **adequately resourced. The reduction of greenhouse gases, financial sector stability, trade openness,** and the responsibility to protect would all be examples of orienting principles. A foreign policy based on an orienting principle is distinct from **pure ad hocery.** It aspires to something beyond specific **short-or medium-term** material interests. A policy that reflects the orienting principle will have a **privileged position with regard to** commanding resources. The orienting principle can be used to **shift** domestic political support even if it fails to create a domestic or international consensus.

Responsible sovereignty is a **potential candidate** for an orienting principle that could guide the policies of the United States and other major powers. The **frame** offered by responsible sovereignty is that effective sovereign states are **a necessary condition** for peace and prosperity both within and among countries. Only if individual states can regulate activities and provide **public services within their own borders** will it be possible to **move towards** greater international order and justice, both by controlling violence within states and concluding **mutually beneficial agreements** among them.

STEPHEN D. KRASNER
http://www.hoover.org

third: (marcador de discurso de enumeração) terceiro, em terceiro lugar
there is ongoing uncertainty: prevalecem incertezas
fourth: (marcador de discurso de enumeração) quarto, em quarto lugar
adequately resourced: receber recursos suficientes
the reduction of greenhouse gases: a redução de gases do efeito estufa
financial sector stability: estabilidade do setor financeiro
trade openness: abertura ao comércio
pure ad hocery: sem qualquer planejamento (do latim "ad hoc")
short- or medium-term: de curto ou médio prazo
privileged position: posição privilegiada
with regard to: com respeito a
shift: mudar, alterar
potential candidate: uma possível opção
frame: modelo, paradigma
a necessary condition: uma condição necessária, pré-requisito
public services: serviços públicos
within their own borders: internamente
move towards: caminhando em direção a
mutually beneficial agreements: acordos mutuamente benéficos

A etimologia da palavra *diplomacy* (diplomacia) vem do grego, *diploma*, que se refere, originalmente, a documentos oficiais, dobrados ao meio e selados. A diplomacia, portanto, estava relacionada ao transporte de tais documentos para efetuar negociações entre cidades-Estado da Antiguidade.

Questions

1. The author suggests that a good "orienting principle" might be:
   a) the end justifies the means
   b) responsible sovereignty
   c) maximize state power at all times
   d) avoid foreign entanglements

2. In the sentence "Grand strategies are designed to *mold* the international environment by regulating international regimes" (line 26), the word "mold" can be replaced correctly by:
   a) shape
   b) challenge
   c) provoke
   d) reconcile
   e) improve

3. Judge each item below.
   According to the author, "grand strategies" fail in the current international environment because:
   a) it is hard to align vision, policies, and resources   (C) (E)
   b) they envision a world that cannot be realized   (C) (E)
   c) resources cannot be aligned with policies   (C) (E)
   d) governments are too weak   (C) (E)

4. Among the challenges of conducting foreign policy under a "grand strategy", the author cites:
   a) acquiring resources (diplomatic, bureaucratic, ideational, military, economic)
   b) having an overarching, articulated vision that can guide policy making in more than just one area
   c) achieving international cooperation
   d) all of the above

5. According to the author, for a "grand strategy" to be successful, it must:
   a) align resources and power
   b) begin with the support of either Germany or the US
   c) align power and beliefs
   d) align resources and beliefs

6 The author proposes that the best alternative to a "grand strategy" is:
   a) altering the opportunity sets of other states
   b) acquiring nuclear weapons
   c) being guided by a set of orienting principles
   d) having no strategy at all

7 The author cites the reduction of greenhouse gasses as an example of:
   a) an orienting principle
   b) a grand strategy
   c) an opportunity set
   d) responsible sovereignty

8 Judge the following items according to the text. The author cites "responsible sovereignty" as being able to do the following:
   a) regulate activities and provide public services within their own borders (C) (E)
   b) control internal violence (C) (E)
   c) reduce poverty (C) (E)
   d) foment economic growth (C) (E)

9 Judge the following items:
   a) on line 16, "norms" could be replaced by "laws" (C) (E)
   b) on line 22, "conceptual" could be replaced by "theoretical" (C) (E)
   c) on line 38, "align" means the same as "dictate" (C) (E)
   d) on line 57, "cleave" means "divide" (C) (E)

4

A usina hidrelétrica de Belo Monte

A aprovação do projeto para construir uma nova usina hidrelétrica em Belo Monte, Pará, repercutiu com intensidade na mídia internacional, em 2010, inclusive nas principais publicações em língua inglesa como The Economist, Financial Times *e* The New York Times. *As publicações internacionais destacaram a enorme escala do projeto, bem como suas consequências sociais, ambientais e econômicas. No artigo reproduzido a seguir, o autor enumera as questões sendo discutidas em relação ao projeto.*

World's third largest hydroelectric plant to be build in Brazil

Thirty years after it was first proposed, a **massive hydroelectric power project** has been approved for the Amazon region. **Once completed**, the Belo Monte Dam will be the world's third-largest hydropower generator after China's *Three Gorges* and southern Brazil's own *Itaipu*. The project involves flooding 500 square kilometers on one of the Amazon River's largest tributaries, the Xingu.

Numerous **complex environmental and social issues have been raised** during the project's **review process**, including the displacement of 16,000 residents, the preservation of lands reserved for **native peoples**, the **destruction of habitat** for **unique fish species**, and even the substantial **carbon and methane emissions** that will come from the **putrefaction** of the flooded forest.

The proposed project also **raises troubling technical and economic questions**. Estimated to

massive: gigante
hydroelectric power project: projeto de construção de uma usina hidrelétrica
once completed: assim que for construída
complex environmental and social issues have been raised: questões sociais e ambientais complexas têm sido levantadas
review process: estudos de viabilidade e de impacto social e ambiental
native peoples: povos indígenas
destruction of habitat: destruição do ecossistema
unique fish species: espécies de peixe únicas
carbon and methane emissions: emissão de dióxido de carbono e de gás metano
putrefaction: apodrecimento, putrefação
raises troubling technical and economic questions: levanta

produce as much as 11 gigawatts, the Belo Monte Dam would theoretically add 10% to the country's **generating capacity**. Engineers, however, calculate that **due to seasonal rainfall variations,** the **plant** should produce, on average, less than half that amount unless additional **upstream dams** are built. Critics argue that this amount of power generation would make the giant dam inefficient.

Due to the **regulatory environment** (**price controls** on the electricity generated), Brazil's largest private construction companies have already **eschewed the project as uneconomic**. This has forced the administration to **sweeten the deal** by **pledging** billions of dollars in **subsidized loans** and **tax incentives**. As the project goes forward, these subsidies will **shift the true costs to the taxpayers**, again raising questions about **cost-effectiveness**.

To be sure, considerations of cost-effectiveness are rare in Brazilian political discourse, especially during election years. The approval of this project **needs to be understood in the context of October's presidential election**, when the **ruling party** (*Lula's Worker's Party*) will seek to **extend power** for another four years. Although it comes only seven months before the election, Belo Monte is **the centerpiece** in the governing party's **public works program**, and promises to generate tens of thousands of direct and indirect jobs in the less developed north. Since voting is not voluntary in Brazil, the link between the current administration and the project should **secure votes** in the region.

The project will also **resonate well with middle class voters farther south,** who for years have complained that government investment in basic services and infrastructure **has not been commensurate with the tax burden**. Although the country's tax burden is relatively high at 40% of **GDP**, and despite a decade of record commodity prices that **filled public coffers**, Brazil's **costly state apparatus** invested little (< 1% of GDP) to improve the country's energy infrastructure. The Belo Monte Dam proposal

questões técnicas e econômicas preocupantes
generating capacity: capacidade de geração de energia
however: (marcador de discurso de oposição) entretanto
due to seasonal rainfall variations: devido às variações sazonais das chuvas
plant: usina
upstream dams: represas adicionais rio acima
regulatory environment: ambiente regulatório, estrutura jurídica
price controls: controle governamental de preços
eschewed the project as uneconomic: rejeitaram o projeto como economicamente inviável
sweeten the deal: melhorar a proposta
pledging: prometendo
subsidized loans: empréstimos subsidiados
tax incentives: incentivos fiscais
shift the true costs to the taxpayers: repassar os custos verdadeiros aos contribuintes
cost-effectiveness: algo que pode ser justificado economicamente pelo custo-benefício (retorno previsto)
to be sure: com certeza
needs to be understood in the context of October's presidential election: tem de ser compreendido no contexto das eleições presidenciais de outubro
ruling party: o partido no poder
extend power: continuar no poder
the centerpiece: o pilar central
public works program: investimentos em infraestrutura (obras públicas)
secure votes: assegurar votos
resonate well with middle class voters farther south: repercutir favoravelmente com os eleitores mais para o sul
has not been commensurate with the tax burden: não tem havido um retorno compatível com a carga tributária
GDP (gross domestic product): PIB (produto interno bruto)
filled public coffers: encheu os

should give a political boost to the governing party in October's elections **whether or not** it **lives up to the rhetoric**.

Daniel Vasconcelos

cofres públicos
costly state apparatus: burocracia estatal custosa
< 1%: (less than one percent) menos de um porcento
should give a political boost to the governing party: deve ser benéfico politicamente para o partido no poder
whether or not: se houver ou não
lives up to the rhetoric: corresponde à altura do discurso oficial

---

Como se compara o Brasil com outros países em termos de produção hidrelétrica?

A Noruega e o Paraguai são os únicos países do mundo que produzem praticamente toda a sua energia elétrica a partir de recursos hídricos. O Brasil produz mais de 85% de sua energia em usinas hidrelétricas. Abaixo, segue uma lista dos maiores produtores, em termos de produção total. A terceira coluna se refere à porcentagem representada pela geração hidrelétrica na economia.

Country	Production (TWh)	Capacity (%)
China	652.05	22.25
Canada	369.50	61.12
Brazil	363.80	85.56
United States	250.60	5.74
Russia	167.00	17.64
Norway	140.50	98.25
India	115.60	15.80
Venezuela	85.96	69.20
Japan	69.20	7.21
Sweden	65.50	44.34

Questions

1 In the title of the article, "largest" is:
   a) a comparative of superiority
   b) a comparative of equality
   c) a comparative of inferiority
   d) a superlative
   e) a comparative of inequality

2   In the sentence "*Once* completed, the Belo Monte Dam will be the world's third-largest hydropower generator", the word "once" can be substituted by:
   a) after being
   b) one time
   c) if
   d) whenever
   e) sometime

3   Judge the following items. According to the author, critics of the hydroelectric project raise the following issues:
   a) the displacement of 16,000 residents   (C) (E)
   b) the preservation of indigenous lands   (C) (E)
   c) the destruction of fish habitats   (C) (E)
   d) carbon emissions   (C) (E)
   e) economic inefficiency   (C) (E)

4   According to the government, how much will the project add to Brazil's generating capacity?
   a) 12%
   b) 10%
   c) 13%
   d) 15%

5   The main point of paragraph 4 is that:
   a) cost-effectiveness is always an important consideration when building infrastructure projects
   b) tax incentives are fundamental for creating viable infrastructure projects
   c) government price controls create distortions that can only be solved with subsidies and other transfers
   d) the government is raising questions about cost-effectiveness

6   In the context of the article, "extend power" (line 42) means:
   a) get elected
   b) transport electricity
   c) get stronger
   d) increase electric production

7   The main point of paragraph 5 is that:
   a) the Belo Monte project is essential for generating new jobs in the north
   b) since taxpayers will assume the costs of Belo Monte, the government shouldn't be concerned with the project's cost-effectiveness

c) despite its inefficiency, the ruling Worker's Party approved the project in order to gain votes in the upcoming election
  d) the economic and environmental costs of the dam will cost the ruling Worker's Party votes in the upcoming election

8 The expression "has not been commensurate with the tax burden" suggests that:
  a) voters feel the government is spending the money well
  b) voters perceive the work as being too costly
  c) voters feel that they are not receiving the services for which they paid
  d) voters wish for lower taxes

9 According to the article, how much does the Brazilian government invest in electricity infrastructure as a percentage of GDP?
  a) less than 1%
  b) more than 1%
  c) 10%
  d) 11%

10 The main purpose of the article is to:
  a) criticize the Brazilian government for proposing absurd projects
  b) raise alarm over the environmental disaster that will follow from building the dam as it is proposed
  c) hypothesize about better alternative energy sources
  d) describe the new government dam proposal and to explore the possible social, political, environmental and economic consequences of that project

11 According to the information provided on the chart after the article, approximately how much of the electric energy requirements of the United States is produced by hydroelectric plants?
  a) 20%
  b) 6%
  c) 50%
  d) 60%

12 Judge the following items.
  a) on line 44 the word "centerpiece" could be correctly replaced with "key program" (C) (E)
  b) on line 15 the word "carbon" refers to "carvão" (C) (E)
  c) on line 58 the word "coffers" is another word for "treasury" (C) (E)
  d) on line 10 the word "issues" refers both to "social" and "environmental" (C) (E)

e) on line 2 "power" can be translated as "potência" and on line 42 as "poder" (C) (E)

f) in the last sentence of the text (line 61), the word "boost" could be correctly replaced by "security" (C) (E)

5

A eleição presidencial de 2010

No artigo a seguir, a professora Zuleika Arashiro, da Universidade de Melbourne, discorre sobre a relevância histórica da eleição presidencial no Brasil em 2010.

Brazilians celebrate a coming of age

At a time when many Western democracies are experiencing a **wave of social conservatism**, Brazilians have used the presidential election to confirm the **transformative power of politics**. Last weekend the **Workers' Party candidate**, economist Dilma Rousseff, was elected president of Brazil. **Ms** Rousseff won 56 per cent (approximately 55.7 million) of votes and defeated the candidate of the **Party of the Brazilian Social Democracy**, José Serra.

The **international coverage** of the elections **highlighted** the fact that Ms Rousseff is the first female president of Brazil. **Indeed**, if there is one **clear message** the majority of Brazilians sent in this election, it is that they are **willing to support change and innovation**, **regardless** of the sex of the candidate. In the **first round** of the presidential election the **Green Party** candidate, **environmental activist** Marina Silva, emerged as the great surprise and captured 20 per cent of votes, much of which would have gone to the Workers' Party in the **final round**.

But the significance of the election **goes beyond** individual performances. Looked at **within the**

coming of age: amadurecimento
wave of social conservatism: onda de conservadorismo
transformative power of politics: força transformadora da política
Workers' Party candidate: candidato do Partido dos Trabalhadores
Ms: pronome de tratamento politicamente correto para mulher que não revela seu estado civil
Party of the Brazilian Social Democracy: Partido da Social Democracia Brasileira (PSDB)
international coverage: cobertura na mídia internacional
highlighted: enfatizou, salientou
indeed: (marcador de discurso usado para dar ênfase) de fato
clear message: mensagem clara
willing to support change and innovation: concordam em apoiar mudança e inovação
regardless: sem levar em consideração
first round: primeiro turno nas eleições
Green Party: Partido Verde
environmental activist: ambientalista

context of South American political history, these elections are a reminder that **participatory democratic politics** has the potential to **fuel social change**.

Although Brazil has been a republic since 1889, its first decades of **electoral politics** were dominated by a mixture of **elite pacts** and efforts to build "the nation" under **heavy state control**. By the 1960s, the legacies of these arrangements were **rigid social stratification** and **extreme inequality**, which left the majority of people without the benefits of the country's wealth. It was the **middle and upper class fear** of an **upheaval among the poor** that helped sustain the military regime between 1964 and 1985.

In those years, Brazilians shared with their South American neighbours the **dark experience of authoritarianism**, with the **absence of rule of law undermining** any notion of **citizenship** and rights. During the Brazilian "economic miracle" of the early 1970s, **annual growth rates** reached 11 per cent, but the price paid by most citizens was a **lack of opportunity** to **break free of their predetermined place in the social order**.

From the mid 1970s the military initiated a slow process of **political liberalisation**. While **labour unions**, the **slum movements** and progressive sectors of the Catholic Church became **well-known actors** in the fight against dictatorship, **ordinary people** also **played a fundamental role**. The campaign for popular presidential elections — Diretas Já ("Direct elections, now") — **gained momentum** in 1984 and **brought millions of Brazilians onto the streets**. Among those actively involved in the campaign were Fernando Henrique Cardoso (president, 1995-98 and 1999-2002), Luiz Inácio Lula da Silva (president, 2003-06 and 2007-10), and Dilma Rousseff.

The **massive popular support** for Diretas Já was one of those moments in history when ordinary people's rejection of the **established order** becomes so intense that it is almost impossible for them to remain silent. The history of South American

---

final round: segundo turno nas eleições
goes beyond: vai além
within the context: no contexto
participatory democratic politics: processo democrático participativo, eleições
fuel social change: promover mudança social
although: embora, apesar de
electoral politics: processo político democrático
elite pacts: arranjos políticos entre as elites
heavy state control: controle estatal rígido e pesado
rigid social stratification: estratificação social rígida
extreme inequality: desigualdade extrema
middle and upper class fear: o medo da classe média e da elite dominante (classe alta)
upheaval among the poor: sublevação ou rebelião dos pobres
dark experience of authoritarianism: experiência sombria do autoritarismo
absence of rule of law: ausência de um Estado de Direito, literalmente: sem lei
undermining: solapando
citizenship: cidadania
annual growth rates: taxas de crescimento anuais
lack of opportunity: falta de oportunidades
break free of their predetermined place in the social order: quebrar as barreiras pré-determinadas na ordem social
political liberalisation: liberalização política
labour unions: sindicatos
slum movements: movimentos populares
well-known actors: participantes bem conhecidos
ordinary people: as pessoas comuns
played a fundamental role: desempenharam um papel fundamental
gained momentum: ganhou impulso

democratisation "from below" provides other inspiring examples: Argentina's mothers and grandmothers of the disappeared **humanised politics** and **infused it with notions of care and compassion**, for example; and the role of the Coalition of Parties for NO in Chile's 1988 referendum gave Chileans an opportunity to reject General Pinochet, surprising conservative forces with an assertion of the courage that years of repression had not eliminated.

In 2002, only two decades after the **darkest period**, Brazilians elected as president the Workers' Party candidate, Luiz Inácio Lula da Silva, a **metalworker** and **labour union leader**. **Free-market ideologues** threatened to punish the country with **capital flight** and **poor investment ratings**. I still remember a sad conversation with a young **expatriate** professional who had decided to move back to the United States. He explained to me that the Brazilian people had made a mistake and warned that we would suffer for it. Now, as we approach the third consecutive Workers' Party administration, Brazil is not only the ninth largest economy in the world but **managed to remain stable even in the face of the 2008 financial crisis**.

It has to be recognised that the **recent social improvements** were **to a great extent** facilitated by the economic stabilisation and **democratic credentials** of the former president, Fernando Henrique Cardoso, from the Party of the Brazilian Social Democracy. **Nevertheless**, the victory of the Workers' Party **revealed a significant change in the Brazilian mindset**. Suddenly, in a society in which the **elite once celebrated opulence and all things European** as **symbols of status**, ordinary Brazilians had reached the **corridors of power**.

Odd political arrangements will undoubtedly continue to emerge, especially in a **multiparty system** in which **political survival is heavily dependent on coalitions**. But considering how recently Brazil moved towards participatory democracy, these tensions are an inevitable part

---

brought millions of Brazilians onto the streets: levou às ruas milhões de brasileiros
massive popular support: apoio popular maciço
established order: a estrutura de poder estabelecida
democratisation "from below": processo democrático que vem das camadas sociais mais populares. Em inglês, usa-se frequentemente a expressão "grass roots" para descrever tais movimentos.
humanised politics: humanizaram a política
infused it with notions of care and compassion: trouxeram os valores de preocupação com os outros e compaixão
darkest period: o período mais sombrio
metalworker: torneiro mecânico
labour union leader: líder de sindicato trabalhista
free-market ideologues: proponentes das ideias do "mercado livre" (a palavra "ideologue" tem um sentido pejorativo)
capital flight: fuga de capitais
poor investment ratings: baixa classificação nos índices de investimentos internacionais
expatriate: expatriado, emigrante
managed to remain stable: conseguiu permanecer estável
even in the face of the 2008 financial crisis: mesmo diante da crise nos mercados financeiros de 2008
recent social improvements: melhorias sociais recentes
to a great extent: em grande parte
democratic credentials: longa trajetória de luta pela democracia
nevertheless: (marcador de discurso para contrastar) mesmo assim
revealed a significant change in the Brazilian mindset: revelou uma mudança significativa nas atitudes dos brasileiros
elite once celebrated opulence and all things European: a elite que uma vez abraçou requintes e tudo que vem da Europa
symbols of status: símbolos de status

of the **creative chaos** that accompanies change. And while **fiscal discipline continues to be the economic mantra**, innovation in social policy has contributed to improvements in **human development indicators**. The Bolsa Família, launched in 2003 and now the world's largest **conditional cash transfer program**, had benefited approximately forty-six million Brazilians by 2008, contributing to a dramatic reduction in poverty from around 34 percent in 2003 to 21.5 percent in 2009. The success of the program has inspired similar **policy initiatives** throughout Latin America and the United States. **Inequality in income distribution**, although still **among the world's highest**, has also decreased. **Moreover, judged by the astonishing support** received by the Green Party's candidate, it would appear that many Brazilians are aware that **environmental sustainability** is a central component of the country's **development agenda**.

Because Brazilians now **enjoy freedom of expression**, and can **gather in public** for all sorts of causes **without the fear of state repression**, it is easy to forget that history and focus on the problems that continue to afflict the country. Corruption, urban violence and a **model of growth** that **struggles to balance business priorities with environmental sustainability**, are still **major challenges**.

Still, the fact that these issues can be openly discussed, and that Brazilian **civil society** now articulates new paths to challenge old concepts of social order, **shows how far society and the state have come in recent decades**.

The "Brazilian model" of democratic development doesn't **fit into quick-and-easy ideological models**. Its **grassroots orientation** makes it dynamic and unpredictable, a complex setting for those who search for **clear-cut answers**. As a Brazilian who **constantly complained** about the country's inability to move from its position of "attractive eternal teenager," for the first time I feel that Brazil has moved into adulthood.

---

corridors of power: bastidores do poder
odd political arrangements: alianças políticas oportunistas
multiparty system: sistema pluripartidário
political survival is heavily dependent on coalitions: a sobrevivência política depende muito da formação de coalizões
creative chaos: desordem criativa
fiscal discipline continues to be the economic mantra: a disciplina fiscal continua sendo a política econômica seguida sem ser questionada
human development indicators: indicadores de desenvolvimento social
conditional cash transfer program: programa assistencialista condicionado
policy initiatives: iniciativas de programas sociais
inequality in income distribution: desigualdade na distribuição de renda
among the world's highest: dentre os maiores do mundo
moreover: (marcador de discurso que acrescenta informação, aditiva) adicionalmente, além disso
judged by the astonishing support: à luz do apoio expressivo
environmental sustainability: preservação do meio ambiente
development agenda: agenda política para o desenvolvimento
enjoy freedom of expression: gozam de liberdade de expressão
gather in public: reunir-se em público
without the fear of state repression: sem medo da repressão estatal
model of growth: modelo de crescimento econômico
struggles to balance business priorities with environmental sustainability: procura equilibrar as prioridades das empresas com a preservação do meio ambiente
major challenges: grandes desafios
still: (marcador de discurso para contrastar) mesmo assim
civil society: sociedade civil

It is too early to know whether we will learn how to **age wisely**. But the results of the 2010 election show that the Workers' Party **campaign slogan** — "so that Brazil will continue to change" — certainly appeals to the Brazilian people at this point in the country's history. In 2010 this nation of 192 million people has more to celebrate than **economic performance**.

ZULEIKA ARASHIRO
http://inside.org.au

shows how far society and the state have come in recent decades: mostra quanto a sociedade e o Estado progrediram nas últimas décadas
fit into quick-and-easy ideological models: encaixa em modelos ideológicos simplistas
grassroots orientation: orientação que vem dos cidadãos comuns
clear-cut answers: respostas claras e concisas
constantly complained: reclamou constantemente
age wisely: envelhecer com sabedoria
campaign slogan: frase publicitária de campanha
economic performance: desempenho da economia

A palavra *candidate* (candidato) aparece originalmente na República Romana quando um cidadão interessado em ser eleito a um cargo público vestia-se em toga branca pintada de cal. Projetava-se assim, com essa vestimenta exageradamente branca, a imagem de alguém que possuía um caráter sem "manchas", imaculado. O adjetivo em latim para "aquele que veste a toga branca" era *candidatus*. Ao longo dos séculos, a palavra passou a ser usada como substantivo para se referir a qualquer pleiteador de cargo público e entrou em uso na língua inglesa no século XVII com esse significado. Etimologicamente, a palavra candidato vem do verbo latim *candere* (luminoso), do qual são derivadas outras palavras como *candid* (cândido, puro), *candor* (pureza, franqueza), *candle* (vela), *candelabra* (castiçal, candelabro), *chandelier* (luminária), and *incandescent* (incandescente).

Questions

1 In the sentence below, "which" refers to:

*In the first round of the presidential election the Green Party candidate, environmental activist Marina Silva, emerged as the great surprise and captured 20 per cent of votes, much of **which** would have gone to the Workers' Party in the final round.*

a) votes
b) the Green Party candidate
c) the first round

d) the presidential election
  e) the Workers' Party victory

2 **Judge the following item:**
  In the sentence below, "they" refers to "majority". (C) (E)

  Indeed, if there is one clear message the majority of Brazilians sent in this election, it is that they are willing to support change and innovation, regardless of the sex of the candidate.

3 **In the sentence "The international coverage of the elections *highlighted* the fact that Ms Rousseff is the first female president of Brazil", the word "highlighted" can be substituted by:**
  a) illuminated
  b) drew attention to
  c) argued
  d) revealed
  e) announced

4 **The author's use of the term *democratisation "from below"* refers to:**
  a) grassroots, popular movements among the lower classes to fight for a more democratic society
  b) democratic movements, independent of social class
  c) the tendency for political power to lie in the hands of the elite
  d) the human rights movement in Latin America in the 1970's

5 **The point the author is trying to make in paragraph 8 is:**
  a) the flight of capital was part of the growth process of Brazil after 2002
  b) the presence of foreign capital and investments in Brazil helped the country to survive the 2008 financial crisis relatively unharmed
  c) in spite of international apprehension over the election of Lula's Worker's Party, Brazil continued to grow and prosper
  d) the Brazilian people had made a mistake and were suffering because of it

6 **In the excerpt "managed to remain stable even in the face of the 2008 financial crisis", the words "even in the face of" could be correctly replaced with "despite" or "in spite of".** (C) (E)

7 **According to the author, which of the following facts about the Bolsa Familia are correct?**
  a) the Bolsa Familia program is the world's largest conditional cash transfer program and by 2009 it had reduced the Brazilian poverty level to 21.5%
  b) the program had benefited 46 million Brazilians by 2008

c) a and b are correct
   d) neither a nor b are correct

8 **The author notes that in spite of recent advances, Brazil is still faced with the following problems:**
   a) corruption, urban violence and environmental degradation
   b) corruption, urban violence and a lack of freedom of expression
   c) a lack of freedom of expression and an inadequate model of growth
   d) state repression

9 **The overall message of the article is:**
   a) that Brazilian politics is dominated by pacts between elite powers
   b) one of pessimism, describing how Brazil can easily return to the authoritarianism it experienced in the 1960's
   c) that the Green Party and the environmental movement are in a position to determine the results of future elections
   d) one of optimism, describing how Brazil has become more democratic and just

A "guerra cambial" entre os Estados Unidos e a China

A chamada "guerra cambial" foi o assunto mais importante na reunião, em 2010, da cúpula do G20, grupo composto pelos países do G8, por 11 países emergentes e pela União Europeia. Com as novas emissões de moeda pelo governo norte-americano, o dólar se deprecia cada vez mais e agrava os problemas comerciais de muitos países. Alguns segmentos industriais no Brasil perderam competitividade internacional no contexto da valorização do real frente ao dólar. Enquanto membros do congresso norte-americano têm acusado a China de manter a sua moeda subvalorizada para assegurar a competitividade de seus produtos no mercado internacional, neste artigo, Eric Margolis argumenta que o governo federal dos EUA adota a mesma estratégia.

China scorns US funny money

1 Washington is **flooding financial markets** with $600 billion of **worthless dollars,** hoping a rising tide of **Monopoly money** will somehow **lift America out of recession. The Fed**'s first **QE** effort was a
5 fizzle. Welcome to **QE2.** In **high finance, hope springs eternal**.

The US government is **stoking worldwide inflation** in order to lower its **outstanding debt** by **repaying creditors** with **depreciated dollars**. The
10 rest of the world is **boiling angry** at Washington.

Just before last week's **G20 economic summit** in South Korea, China's state credit agency **publicly downgraded America's credit rating** and questioned US leadership of the world's economy.

scorns: rejeita, desdenha, despreza
funny money: dinheiro falso (informal)
flooding financial markets: inundando os mercados financeiros
worthless dollars: dólares sem valor
monopoly money: dinheiro de brincadeira, como usado no jogo Banco Imobiliário
lift America out of recession: estimular a economia americana a sair da recessão
the Fed: forma abreviado do nome do banco central norte-americano (Federal Reserve), sempre usado com o artigo "the"
QE: (acrônimo de "quantitative easing") "relaxamento quantitativo", a impressão de moeda pelo banco

In an unprecedented, **stinging rebuke**, China scolded Washington for "**deteriorating debt repayment capability**", and predicted quantitative easing would lead to "fundamentally **lowering the national solvency**".

This was a real **slap in the face** heard **around the globe** — particularly coming from **a bunch of commies**! China is the **largest holder of US government debt**.

I remember the day when my father, a New York **financier**, used to **sneer at iffy stock or bond issues** as, "Chinese paper." Now, it's "American paper." **How the world has turned**.

Washington has been blasting China for **manipulating its currency** to keep the value low — which is quite true. Embarrassingly, Germany and Brazil just accused the US of being as big a currency manipulator as China — which is also quite true. The EU refused to join the US in alone blaming China for **world financial and currency instability**.

A depreciated dollar boosts US exports and hurts nations exporting to the US. Economists call it, "**beggar thy neighbor**", a destructive trade practice that **played a key role** in the 1930's world depression.

This **money flood** is **eroding the value of the dollar**, the **world's premier medium of exchange**. In the past two months, the US dollar has dropped 6% against other major currencies. **Frightened investors are piling into gold**, now up 17% in 60 days.

The Obama administration, just **"shellacked" by voters** in **midterm elections**, and desperate to lower unemployment, is **gambling more debt shock therapy will spark the economy back to life**. But massive, unsustainable debt caused the US **financial meltdown** in 2008.

The **US public debt** has hit a stratospheric $14 trillion. You don't treat a poisoning victim with more poison. **Spending one's way to prosperity** with borrowed money is a **dangerous chimera**. But **panicky politicians** are ready to try any sort of **economic snake oil remedy** to **save their skins**.

---

central norte-americano
fizzle: fracasso
QE2: (acrônimo de "quantitative easing two") uma segunda proposta de imprimir e lançar grande quantidade de moeda pelo banco central norte-americano
high finance: altas finanças
hope springs eternal: nunca se perde a esperança
stoking worldwide inflation: fomentando a inflação global
outstanding debt: dívidas
repaying creditors: ressarcindo os credores
depreciated dollars: dólares depreciados
boiling angry: furioso
G20 economic summit: reunião econômica dos países no grupo G20
publicly downgraded America's credit rating: rebaixou publicamente a avaliação em relação à capacidade do governo americano em pagar suas dívidas
stinging rebuke: forte repreensão, exprobração
deteriorating debt repayment capability: uma capacidade deteriorada de ressarcir os credores
lowering the national solvency: diminuindo a capacidade do Estado de saldar dívidas
slap in the face: tapa na cara, injúria, insulto (informal)
around the globe: internacionalmente, ao redor do mundo
a bunch of commies: um bando de comunistas (usado com efeito humorístico)
largest holder of US government debt: o país que mais possui títulos do governo norte-americano
financier: homem das altas finanças
sneer at iffy stock or bond issues: menosprezava ações e bônus de fontes questionáveis
how the world has turned: como o mundo mudou
Washington has been blasting China: Washington tem fortemente criticado a China
manipulating its currency: manipulando a sua moeda

Before 2007, America was **living high on phony financial froth**. **Finance** had become America's **leading business**. Those days are over but **no one dares to tell the voters**.

Besides destabilizing **world exchange rates** and **trade**, Washington's money flood is **pouring into emerging markets** as American investors **seek higher returns** than the **miserable pittance** available at home, creating **highly volatile capital flows**.

The **so-called financial rescue package** brought in by Presidents Bush and Obama **have been a bonanza** for **Wall Street** and the banks, and a **catastrophe for savers and ordinary citizens**.

During the 1980's, we saw fragile Asian economies **battered** as **investment from the US flooded in, then out**. This is happening again, **boosting currencies** of many nations, making their exports uncompetitive. **Investment barriers** are going up from China to Brazil.

President Barack Obama **inherited a horrible mess** from the Bush administration. **However**, his **wrongheaded economic response** is **undermining the world's economic order**. A nation's currency is more a symbol of its strength and **good name** than its flag. **Running down the US dollar**, which ruled world finance since 1945, could mark the **beginning of the end** of the American era.

That's what the American delegation to the G20 economic summit in Seoul, South Korea and Yokohama, Japan, heard last weekend. Obama's **economic policies**, notably his attempts to **stimulate the US economy with the steroids of more deficit spending**, were **roundly rejected and criticized** by other G20 members. **No decisions were reached** on **exchange rates**.

However, there was an **uncommon flash of common sense** in Washington last week. A special **bipartisan presidential panel on reducing the national deficit** proposed $4 trillion in **federal spending cuts**.

world financial and currency instability: a instabilidade financeira e monetária internacional
a depreciated dollar boosts US exports: o dólar depreciado aumenta as exportações norte-americanas
beggar thy neighbor: estratégia de empobrecer o seu vizinho num jogo de soma zero
played a key role: desempenhou um papel fundamental
money flood: enxurrada de [nova] moeda
eroding the value of the dollar: está destruindo o valor do dólar
world's premier medium of exchange: a moeda padrão no comércio internacional
frightened investors are piling into gold: investidores amedrontados estão comprando ouro em grande escala
"shellacked" by voters: surrado nas urnas
midterm elections: eleições legislativas dois anos após o começo do mandato presidencial norte-americano
gambling more debt shock therapy will spark the economy back to life: apostando que uma terapia de choque de endividamento poderá reanimar a economia
financial meltdown: colapso do sistema financeiro
US public debt: dívida pública norte-americana
spending one's way to prosperity: gastando até alcançar a prosperidade
dangerous chimera: mito perigoso
panicky politicians: políticos apavorados
economic snake oil remedy: uma falsa e "milagrosa" cura econômica
save their skins: salvarem-se
living high on phony financial froth: gozando de uma abundância ou riqueza ilusória
finance: a área financeira
leading business: indústria mais importante
no one dares to tell the voters: ninguém se arrisca a dizê-lo aos eleitores

All **political sacred cows** were targeted. The biggest: the monstrous $700 billion **military budget**. A third of US worldwide military bases would close. There would be cuts to **social security**, **mortgage deductions**, delays in retirement age, an end to politician's local **pet projects**. Taxes would rise.

The **howling** has already begun. Unfortunately, such unpopular, **drastic spending cuts seem highly unlikely**, particularly in the new US Congress where Republicans and Democrats will be **deadlocked**. America would need an economic dictator to implement the panel's full plan.

China has one — the Communist Party. America does not and is **rudderless. More empires have been undone by financial collapse than invasion** or battlefield defeats. The **once mighty** United States is **staggering in this direction.**

Eric Margolis
www.lewrockwell.com

world exchange rates: taxas de câmbio internacionais
trade: comércio
pouring into emerging markets: indo em grandes quantidades aos mercados emergentes
seek higher returns: procuram retornos mais elevados
miserable pittance: quantia pequeno, mixaria
highly volatile capital flows: fluxos de capitais altamente voláteis
so-called: suposto, chamado (usado de forma irônica)
financial rescue package: pacote de ajuda ao sistema financeiro
have been a bonanza: tem sido altamente lucrativos
Wall Street: setor financeiro norte-americano, localizado na cidade de Nova Iorque
catastrophe for savers and ordinary citizens: catástrofe para os poupadores e os cidadãos comuns

battered: surradas
investment from the US flooded in, then out: investimentos (financeiros) entraram e saíram em grande escala e velocidade
boosting currencies: (super) valorizando moedas
investment barriers: barreiras aos investimentos (especificamente aos capitais especulativos)
inherited a horrible mess: herdou uma tremenda confusão, herdou grandes problemas
however: (marcador de discurso para contrastar) entretanto
wrongheaded economic response: respostas governamentais equivocadas
undermining the world's economic order: solapando a ordem econômica internacional
good name: boa reputação
running down the US dollar: rebaixando o valor do dólar norte-americano

beginning of the end: o começo do fim
economic policies: políticas econômicas
stimulate the US economy with the steroids of more deficit spending: estimular a economia artificialmente com gastos deficitários ("steroids" são anabolizantes, fármacos que estimulam o crescimento muscular)
roundly rejected and criticized: amplamente rejeitado e criticado
no decisions were reached: não houve decisão
exchange rates: taxas de câmbio
uncommon flash of common sense: momento de extraordinária lucidez, de senso comum
bipartisan presidential panel on reducing the national deficit: painel presidencial com membros dos dois maiores partidos para reduzir a dívida pública federal
federal spending cuts: cortes nos gastos federais
political sacred cows: programas políticos considerados politicamente intocáveis
military budget: orçamento militar
social security: programa de apoio social
mortgage deductions: isenção de imposto sobre hipotecas
pet projects: projetos favoritos
howling: uivos, gritos
drastic spending cuts seem highly unlikely: grandes cortes parecem ser altamente improváveis
deadlocked: sem acordo, travado politicamente
rudderless: sem direção, literalmente sem leme
more empires have been undone by financial collapse than invasion: mais impérios caíram devido a colapsos financeiros do que devido a invasões
once mighty: que foi uma vez forte
staggering in this direction: titubeando nessa direção

Durante a reunião do G20, a BBC comentou que o ministério das relações exteriores da China fez uma solicitação formal à delegação inglesa no sentido de não usar a flor de papoula em suas lapelas. Muitos ingleses usam essa flor no mês de novembro em homenagem àqueles que morreram na Primeira Guerra Mundial. Para os chineses, entretanto, a flor de papoula carrega uma conotação negativa, especialmente associada aos ingleses. A papoula é a matéria-prima do ópio, e, durante o século XIX, o império britânico perpetrou duas guerras contra a China, chamadas de "guerras do ópio". Para os chineses a papoula traz lembranças da opressão imperial inglesa no século XIX.

Questions

1. The sentence "China's state credit agency publicly downgraded America's credit rating" (line 12) means:
   a) China is confident that the US can pay its debts
   b) China publicly questions the US government's ability to repay its debts
   c) the US cannot borrow money from China in the future
   d) the US will default on its debt payments to China
   e) the world doesn't trust the US

2. On line 28, the word "blasting" could best be substituted by:
   a) exploding
   b) requesting
   c) observing
   d) admiring
   e) criticizing

3. The word "boosts", in the sentence "A depreciated dollar *boosts* US exports" (line 35), could be correctly replaced by:
   a) increases
   b) hurts
   c) lowers
   d) adds value to
   e) makes more attractive

4. According to the article, the total American public debt is:
   a) 14 trillion dollars
   b) 14 billion dollars

c) not an important consideration
   d) 10 trillion dollars

5 In the sentence *"Running down* the US dollar, which ruled world finance since 1945, could mark the beginning of the end of the American era", the phrasal verb "running down" means:
   a) criticizing severely
   b) spending
   c) devaluing
   d) saving
   e) chasing

6 With regards to "quantitative easing" the author of the article believes that:
   a) it is one of many viable measures to stimulate the American economy
   b) President Obama had no choice but to print more money to save the American economy
   c) it has been largely successful so far and will probably keep America from falling into a deep recession
   d) it will hurt America, lead to further devaluation of the US dollar and possibly a general collapse of the American economy
   e) it will lead to a stronger US dollar and hurt American exports

7 The 4 trillion in spending cuts proposed by the bipartisan presidential panel include cuts to all except one of the following:
   a) education
   b) social security
   c) the military budget
   d) reduction of overseas military bases
   e) delaying the retirement age

8 Which of the following best describes the main point of the article:
   a) China will devaluate its own currency to compete with the dollar causing a spiral of inflation
   b) the dollar is worth only a fraction of what it was worth only a few decades ago
   c) American military spending is too costly and drains too many resources
   d) the intentional devaluation of the US dollar, which is the root cause of worldwide inflation, is being questioned by China

7

A declaração diplomática brasileira contra sanções ao Irã

Em 2010, o governo brasileiro declarou, no Conselho de Segurança das Nações Unidas, sua oposição à adoção de novas sanções contra o Irã. Brasil e Turquia foram os únicos dos 15 membros do Conselho a votar contra a aplicação de sanções. Nessa ocasião, a embaixadora do Brasil argumentou que experiências recentes demonstram que, além de serem ineficazes, sanções podem trazer consequências perversas. A posição adotada foi consistente com a tradição da política exterior brasileira que procura solucionar disputas internacionais de forma pacífica e negociada.

Brazilian declaration on Iran at the UN

1   Brazil has voted against the **draft resolution**. In doing so, we are **honouring the purposes** that inspired us in the efforts that resulted in the **Tehran Declaration** of 17 May.
5   We do not see sanctions as an **effective instrument** in this case. Sanctions will most probably lead to the suffering of the people of Iran and will **play in the hands** of those, on all sides, that do not want **dialogue to prevail**.
10   Past experiences in the UN, notably the case of Iraq, show that the **spiral of sanctions, threats and isolation** can result in **tragic consequences**.
    We voted against [sanctions] also because the adoption of sanctions, **at this juncture**, runs
15 **contrary to** the successful efforts of Brazil and

UN: abreviação de United Nations (Organização das Nações Unidas)
draft resolution: proposta de resolução
honouring the purposes: agindo de acordo com o propósito
Tehran Declaration: uma declaração conjunta controversa do Brasil, Turquia e Irã propondo a troca de materiais nucleares
effective instrument: instrumento eficaz
play in the hands: favorecer um ponto de vista (a expressão correta seria "play into the hands of someone")
dialogue to prevail: que o diálogo prevaleça
spiral of sanctions, threats and isolation: espiral de sanções,

53

Turkey to engage Iran in a **negotiated solution** for its **nuclear programme**.

As Brazil **repeatedly stated**, the Tehran Declaration adopted 17 May is a **unique opportunity that should not be missed**. It was **approved by the highest levels** of the Iranian leadership and endorsed by its Parliament.

The Tehran Declaration **promoted a solution that would ensure the full exercise of Iran's right** to the peaceful use of nuclear energy, while providing full **verifiable assurances** that Iran's nuclear programme has exclusively **peaceful purposes**.

We are **firmly convinced** that the only possible way to achieve this **collective goal** is to secure Iran's cooperation through effective and **action-oriented dialogue** and negotiations.

The Tehran Declaration showed that dialogue and persuasion can do more than **punitive actions**. Its purpose and result were to **build the confidence** needed to **address a whole set of** aspects of Iran's nuclear programme.

As we explained yesterday, the Joint Declaration removed **political obstacles** to the materialization of a proposal by the IAEA in October 2009. Many governments and highly respected institutions and individuals **have come to acknowledge** its value as an important step to a **broader discussion** on the Iranian nuclear program.

The Brazilian government **deeply regrets**, therefore, that the Joint Declaration has **neither received the political recognition it deserves, nor** been given the time it needs to **bear fruit**.

Brazil considers it **unnatural** to rush to sanctions before the **parties concerned** can sit and talk about the implementation of the Declaration. The Vienna Group's replies to the Iranian letter of 24 May, which confirmed Iran's commitment to the contents of the Declaration, were received just hours ago. No time has been given for Iran to react to the opinions of the Vienna Group, including to the proposal of a technical meeting to **address** details.

---

ameaças e isolamento
tragic consequences: consequências trágicas
at this juncture: neste momento
runs contrary to: é contrária a, contraria
negotiated solution: solução negociada
nuclear programme: programa nuclear
repeatedly stated: ressaltou em várias ocasiões
unique opportunity that should not be missed: oportunidade única que não deve ser desperdiçada
approved by the highest levels: foi aprovada nos mais altos escalões
promoted a solution that would ensure the full exercise of Iran's right: promoveu uma solução que iria assegurar plenamente os direitos do Irã
verifiable assurances: meios seguros de verificar
peaceful purposes: propósitos pacíficos
firmly convinced: totalmente convencidos
collective goal: objetivo coletivo
action-oriented dialogue: diálogo com objetivos práticos
punitive actions: ações punitivas
build the confidence: aumentar a confiança
address: abordar, lidar com
a whole set of: um conjunto de
political obstacles: obstáculos políticos
have come to acknowledge: vieram a reconhecer
broader discussion: discussão mais ampla
deeply regrets: lamenta profundamente
neither... nor: (marcador de discurso disjuntivo) nem... nem
received the political recognition it deserves: recebeu o reconhecimento político que merecia
bear fruit: mostrar resultados
unnatural: impróprio, descabido, ilógico
parties concerned: os grupos envolvidos

The adoption of sanctions in such circumstances **sends the wrong signal** to what could be the beginning of a **constructive engagement** in Vienna.

It was also a **matter of grave concern** the way in which the permanent members, together with a country that is not a member of the **Security Council**, negotiated **among themselves** for months **behind closed doors**.

For all these reasons, Brazil does not believe that this is the moment to adopt further sanctions against Iran.

We believe, along with many, that the only viable solution to disagreements with Iran over its nuclear program is a **negotiated diplomatic solution**. This is why we are convinced that the **fuel exchange arrangement** of last May is an opportunity that should not be missed.

www.globalresearch.ca

address: tratar de, lidar com
sends the wrong signal: inviabiliza, manda uma mensagem contraproducente
constructive engagement: diálogo ou engajamento construtivo
matter of grave concern: assunto seriíssimo
Security Council: Conselho de Segurança das Nações Unidas
among themselves: entre si
behind closed doors: em segredo

negotiated diplomatic solution: solução diplomática negociada
fuel exchange arrangement: acordo sobre troca de materiais nucleares

---

Algumas palavras em inglês originárias da língua persa: *candy* (doce), *carafe* (garrafa), *caravan* (caravana), *caviar* (caviar), *cushy* (fácil, confortável), *Mussulman* (muçulmano), *pajama* (pijama), *paradise* (paraíso, cidade cercada), *pistachio* (pistache), *satrap* (sátrapa, grande senhor), *serendipity* (serendipidade, descoberta afortunada), *shah* (rei, xá), *spinach* (espinafre), *sugar* (açúcar), *talc* (talco), *tambour* (tambor).

Questions

1 The modal verb "will" in the sentence "Sanctions *will* most probably lead to the suffering of the people of Iran and *will* play in the hands of those, on all sides, that do not want dialogue to prevail." expresses:
   a) certainty
   b) possibility
   c) permission
   d) obligation
   e) uncertainty

2 We can infer from the text that the expression "tragic consequences" (line 12) refers to:
   a) reaching a permanent political impasse
   b) a situation of war may ensue as was the case in Iraq
   c) bureaucrats losing their jobs
   d) a spiral of sanctions
   e) a breakdown in negotiations

3 Judge the following:
   a) the Brazilian government is satisfied with the response of other nations regarding the Joint Declaration (C) (E)
   b) the Brazilian government feels more time is necessary for the Joint Declaration to be successful (C) (E)

4 In the excerpt below "themselves" refers to both "permanent members" and "a country that is not a member of the Security Council". (C) (E)

   *It was also a matter of grave concern the way in which the permanent members, together with a country that is not a member of the Security Council, negotiated among **themselves** for months behind closed doors.*

5 Judge the following:
   a) on line 14 the expression "runs contrary to" could be correctly replaced by "is not compatible with" (C) (E)
   b) on line 48 the word "unnatural" could be correctly replaced by "supernatural" (C) (E)
   c) on line 64 the expression "among themselves" could be correctly replaced by "between themselves" (C) (E)
   d) on line 33 the expression "punitive actions" could be correctly replaced by the word "sanctions" (C) (E)

6 The objective of the author is to persuade other nations to pursue a path of negotiation with Iran. To that end, the text makes frequent use of emotional appeals. (C) (E)

7 The main purpose of the article is to:
   a) justify and defend why Brazil doesn't want to adopt sanctions against Iraq
   b) convince the UN to drop sanctions against Iraq
   c) explain why sanctions don't work
   d) persuade the US to join Brazil in a shared diplomatic effort
   e) warn the general public about problems in Iraq

Direitos de propriedade e subdesenvolvimento

James Robinson é professor de administração pública na Universidade de Harvard, onde pesquisa questões acerca do desenvolvimento econômico. Neste artigo, o professor Robinson tece argumentos sobre a importância do direito de propriedade na criação de riquezas.

Property rights and African poverty

1 One of the **burning intellectual and policy issues** of our day is the poverty in **sub-Saharan Africa**, attracting the attention of everyone from **entrepreneurs** such as Bill Gates through movie
5 stars such as Madonna and Angelina Jolie to rock stars such as Bono and Bob Geldof. The **World Bank** measures **poverty levels** by the number of people who **live on less than $1 a day**; the majority of those people, around 350 million of them, live in
10 sub-Saharan Africa. **Moreover**, Africa is the only part of the world in which the **absolute number** of poor people is increasing. By 2015, despite all the attention given to the **United Nations' Millennium Development Goals**, the number of poor people in
15 Africa is forecast to be more than 400 million.
    Why are there so many poor people in Africa today? Has Africa always been like this? There are many **differing views**. Some see African poverty as having **deep roots** in the geography and ecology of
20 the continent. Others argue that Africa is **plagued by a culture that does not allow capitalism to flourish**. I argue in this essay that the real reason

property rights: direitos de propriedade
burning intellectual and policy issues: assuntos políticos e intelectuais mais importantes
sub-Saharan Africa: África subsaariana
entrepreneurs: empreendedores
World Bank: Banco Mundial
poverty levels: níveis de pobreza
live on less than $1 a day: sobrevivem com menos de um dólar por dia
moreover: (marcador de discurso que acrescenta informação) adicionalmente, além disso
absolute number: número absoluto
United Nations' Millennium Development Goals: as Metas de Desenvolvimento do Milênio (MDM) surgem da Declaração do Milênio das Nações Unidas, adotada em 2000
differing views: pontos de vista diferentes
deep roots: raízes profundas
plagued by a culture that does not allow capitalism to flourish:

that Africa has been poor historically and is poor today has to do with property rights. **In short,** African countries do not have the same type of property rights that are connected with economic progress in Western Europe or North America. And the property rights they do have **tend to be insecure.**

The form of property rights in Africa — and their absence, in many cases — is the **root source** of its poverty, which creates both good and bad news. The good news is that Africa is not **doomed to poverty**; if its property rights institutions can be improved, Africa will grow and its people's **living standards** will improve. The bad news is that there is no **silver bullet** for improving property rights. For example, **throwing aid money at Africa** may alleviate suffering but is unlikely to improve its institutions. **Worse,** many of the problems with property rights in Africa **stem from** problems with politics and political institutions; these problems are **not easy for either insiders or outsiders to fix.** Africa is not doomed to poverty, if its property rights institutions can be improved.

When examining the **role of property rights** in African poverty, we should begin by looking at its history. We know that, before the **Industrial Revolution** began in Great Britain about two hundred thirty years ago, differences in the **levels of prosperity** among countries were much smaller than they are now. **Whereas** today the **average income** of a citizen of the United States is about **forty times** that of a citizen of a country such as Ethiopia or Sierra Leone, in 1750 that difference was probably only two or three. Between 1750 and 2009, the United States experienced **rapid economic growth,** but African countries did not. Even in 1750, **however,** there were important differences in the structures of the various societies. Although we don't know when many of those differences emerged, we can **open some windows on the past.**

In **500 AD,** for example, **the Kingdom of Aksum flourished in northern Ethiopia**; it had a written language, **minted its own coins,** and **enjoyed a**

---

coibido ou restringido por uma cultura que não permite o capitalismo a florescer

in short: (marcador de discurso para resumir ou concluir) em suma, em resumo

tend to be insecure: tendem a ser precários, inseguros, não confiáveis

root source: fonte, causa

doomed to poverty: condenados a (uma vida de) pobreza

living standards: padrões de vida

silver bullet: solução fácil

throwing aid money at Africa: gastar grandes quantidades de dinheiro em África (para fins humanitários)

worse: pior ainda

stem from: tem origem em

not easy for either insiders or outsiders to fix: não são fáceis nem para os nativos nem para pessoas de fora resolverem

role of property rights: papel desempenhado pelo direito de propriedade

Industrial Revolution: Revolução Industrial

levels of prosperity: níveis de riqueza

whereas: (marcador de discurso para contrastar) enquanto, ao passo que

average income: renda média

forty times: quarenta vezes

rapid economic growth: crescimento econômico acelerado

however: (marcador de discurso para contrastar) entretanto

open some windows on the past: explorar a história, entender o passado

500 AD: 500 anos depois de Cristo (AD refere-se a "anno domini")

the Kingdom of Aksum flourished in northern Ethiopia: o Reino de Aksum prosperou no norte da Etiópia

minted its own coins: cunhou suas próprias moedas

diversified agricultural economy based on ox-drawn plows. The kingdom traded with the eastern Mediterranean, the Persian Gulf and the Arabian Peninsula, India, and Sri Lanka. The Roman emperor Constantine converted to Christianity in 312 AD; Ezana, the king of Aksum, did so in 333 AD, a mere twenty-one years later.

Nevertheless, in both technology and the development of political institutions, Africa's trajectory seems to have been different from Western Europe's. Outside Ethiopia, **neither the plow nor the wheel** was used in sub-Saharan Africa; the great urban centers of Aksum and Mali **seem to have been the exception rather than the rule**. Moreover, the political institutions of both these societies could best be described as "absolutist" **in that** they were ruled by kings whose power was relatively **unconstrained by checks and balances**.

The economic problems created by absolutism are well illustrated by the history of the Kingdom of the Kongo (in what is now the Democratic Republic of the Congo, which took its name from the pre-modern kingdom). The capital of the Kongo, Mbanza, had a population of around sixty thousand when it was first visited by the Portuguese mariner Diogo Cão in 1483, making Mbanza about the same size as Lisbon and larger than London, which had a population of about fifty thousand in 1500.

The Kongolese learned about plows and wheels from the Portuguese, who sent missions in 1491 and 1512 to **encourage better agricultural practices**. Yet neither the plow nor the wheel was **widely used** until **early in the twentieth century**. We learn why from existing accounts of how the society was organized. The Kongo was governed by a king and an aristocracy whose wealth was **based on slave plantations and the extraction of taxes**. Slavery, which was central to the economy, was practiced by the elite both to supply their own plantations and to sell to Europeans at the coast. Taxes were arbitrary (one was collected every time the king's beret fell off).

To have become more prosperous, the Kongolese would need to have **saved and invested in plows**, for example. But this would not have been worthwhile in that any extra output they produced by using plows and wheels would have been **expropriated by the king and his lords**. Most people's property rights were also highly insecure; many moved their villages away from roads so as to reduce the incidence of **plunder**.

Aksum and its successor, Ethiopia, may not have looked very different from contemporary European societies in 500 AD, even developing a form of feudalism at the same time as Europe did. Yet after this point, very **different institutional dynamics took hold** and the property rights institutions of Western Europe began to diverge from those of Africa. In Europe, **domestic slavery** had disappeared by 1400; around the same time, feudal institutions such as **serfdom began to crumble**. Both institutions continued in Ethiopia until the **mid-twentieth century**.

As eighteenth-century British historian Edward Gibbon (author of The Decline and Fall of the Roman Empire) put it, the Ethiopians "slept near a thousand years." But something very different was happening in Britain. Not only did **labor market institutions** and property rights for people change, so did property rights in ideas and people's access to land change. The 1623 Statute of Monopolies created the world's first **patent law**; as serfdom **eroded**, **private property rights** in land developed. Those institutions, which subsequently spread to some European colonies, including the future United States, created a radically different set of economic incentives in Britain.

Why did this happen in Britain but not in the Kongo or Ethiopia? Interestingly, the motivation behind the Statute of Monopolies was not to create a patent law but to stop the king from granting monopolies via "letters patent." **Thus** the creation of a law that ultimately protected **intellectual property rights** and stimulated innovation was a **by-product**

---

saved and invested in plows: poupado e investido em arados

expropriated by the king and his lords: expropriado (confiscado) pelo rei e pela nobreza

plunder: roubo

different institutional dynamics took hold: vingaram novas dinâmicas institucionais

domestic slavery: escravidão no país

serfdom began to crumble: o sistema de servidão feudal começou a se desintegrar

mid-twentieth century: meados do século vinte

labor market institutions: instituições relacionadas ao mercado de trabalho, trabalhistas

patent law: lei de patentes
eroded: entrou em declínio
private property rights: direito de propriedade particular

thus: (marcador de discurso de conclusão) logo, portanto, então, por isso, por conseguinte, por isto, assim

intellectual property rights: direito de propriedade intelectual

by-product: consequência

of the conflict between Parliament and the king, an attempt by Parliament to defeat absolutism.

The political conflicts of seventeenth-century Britain, through the Civil War of the 1640s to the Glorious Revolution of 1688, removed the type of absolutist political rule that led to insecure property rights in the Kongo and Ethiopia. Indeed, we can see the political transition of Britain beginning with the decline of serfdom in the fourteenth century. After the **Black Death** of the 1340s, the English state passed the Statute of Laborers, an attempt to **stop wages from rising**. The ensuing rebellion **forced the king to rescind the statute**, evidence that he lacked the power to enforce it.

Foreign policy toward Africa **has been driven** too much by short-term politics not focused on economic development. Britain, then, was on a very different political trajectory, one with huge consequences for property rights and prosperity. The kings of the Kongo and Ethiopia also faced domestic opponents, but they were unable to triumph; even if they had, they most likely would have become absolutist kings themselves. What is distinctive about the British experience is not just that absolutism was defeated but that one absolutism was not replaced by another.

What explains the rise of Parliament and the defeat of absolutism in Britain? Why did the rise of Parliament create changes in economic institutions? The answer is that British society **had undergone a series of large shocks** that not only greatly increased the number of those with an interest in secure property rights but also **empowered** them.

Even more important than the early shock of the Black Death was the redistribution of land brought on by Henry VIII's dissolution of the monasteries after 1536, the enormous economic opportunities created by the **New World**, and the expansion of **interoceanic trade** after 1492. The Whigs who fought and defeated absolutism in 1688 did so to change state policy and institutions in ways that would promote their economic interests. Because their coalition was so broad, what they wanted would

---

Black Death: peste bulbônica, peste negra

stop wages from rising: impedir que salários aumentassem

forced the king to rescind the statute: forçou o rei a revogar o estatuto (lei)

foreign policy: política exterior
has been driven: foi impelida por, guiou-se por

had undergone a series of large shocks: havia passado por uma série de grandes mudanças

empowered: "empoderou" (refere-se à capacidade de os indivíduos e grupos poderem decidir sobre as questões que lhes concernem)

New World: o Novo Mundo, as Américas
interoceanic trade: comércio marítimo interoceânico, entre vários continentes

benefit society **as a whole**, with no going back to absolutism. The institutions that protected the privileges of the king at the expense of his subjects, and that allocated monopoly rights for **profitable lines of businesses** to the elite aligned with the king, were **torn down**, to be replaced by institutions providing much greater **incentives to save, invest, and innovate** for a larger slice of society.

It is no coincidence that Britain's Industrial Revolution began within a century of the Glorious Revolution of 1688 and the ascendance of modern **parliamentary democracy** over the monarchy. The great inventors — such as Richard Trevithick, builder of the first full-scale working railway steam locomotive; James Watt, the Scottish mechanical engineer and inventor; Richard Arkwright, the mechanical engineer credited with using water power for spinning machines; and Isambard Kingdom Brunel, a British engineer whose designs revolutionized public transportation — were able to **take advantage of** the economic opportunities generated by their ideas, secure in the knowledge that their property rights would be respected.

The **political developments** in Britain that led to secure property rights and widespread economic opportunities were the **outcome** of conflict and the defeat of absolutism. The same was true in the United States; good British institutions were not transmitted to the Jamestown colony. **For one thing**, British institutions were not yet fully established in 1607. **For another**, the model of colonization that the settlers had in mind was inspired by Spanish conquistadores Hernán Cortés and Francisco Pizarro: capture the ruler and exploit the indigenous people. But such a strategy was **infeasible** in the colonies; by 1619, the Virginia Company, having given up trying to exploit both indigenous peoples and colonists, created a general assembly based on **universal male suffrage**.

Give Africans more economic opportunities, not by **throwing money at them** but by **opening markets** to African exports and **trade**.

---

as a whole: como um todo, de uma forma geral

profitable lines of businesses: áreas de comércio lucrativas

torn down: derrubados

incentives to save, invest, and innovate: incentivos para poupar, investir e inovar

parliamentary democracy: democracia parlamentarista

take advantage of: aproveitar de

political developments: mudanças políticas

outcome: resultado

for one thing: (marcador de discurso para enumerar) em primeiro lugar

for another: (marcador de discurso para enumerar) em segundo lugar, adicionalmente

infeasible: inviável

universal male suffrage: sufrágio (direito de voto) para todos os homens

throwing money at them: dar-lhes dinheiro cegamente

opening markets: abrindo mercados

trade: comércio

As British North America developed, British elites tried **time and again** to create a relatively oligarchic society with heavily restricted economic and political rights for the **vast mass of individuals**. In each case **this model broke down**, just as it had in Virginia, because, as in Britain itself, those with an interest in secure property rights and widespread economic opportunities **gained the upper hand**, though they did so for different reasons than in Britain itself. In the New World, where land was plentiful and labor scarce, the mass of people had power because they did not rely on elites for access to economic opportunities. Instead, the elite had to rely on the people. Such early conflicts created a society with **widely dispersed** political and property rights in which economic opportunities were probably more widespread than anywhere else in the world at that time, culminating in the U.S. Constitution and the economic success of the United States in the nineteenth and twentieth centuries.

African institutional dynamics were very different. In Ethiopia was isolation and **stasis**; elsewhere, the insecurity of property rights was exacerbated by the **slave trade**, which distorted paths of political development and led to the emergence of states, such as the Kongo, based not on investing but on slavery. Africa's increasing **economic backwardness** made it vulnerable to colonialism, which replaced one form of absolutism with another. Later, independence did the same, with predictable consequences for property rights.

A good example of this is Sierra Leone, whose status as a British colony emphasizes that there was no advantage in such status. Six years after independence in 1961, Sierra Leone was taken over by Siaka Stevens, who **pulled up the railway line** to the south of the country and sold off all the **track and rolling stock** to isolate the Mendeland region where support for his opposition was strongest. The **roads fell to pieces** and schools disintegrated. **National television broadcasts** stopped in 1987. The **Sierra Leone Produce Marketing Board** expropriated

---

time and again: muitas vezes

vast mass of individuals: grande maioria das pessoas

this model broke down: este modelo se esgotou

gained the upper hand: ganhou posição de vantagem

widely dispersed: amplamente distribuídas

stasis: estagnação

slave trade: comércio de escravos

economic backwardness: atraso econômico

pulled up the railway line: desmanchou a linha ferroviária

track and rolling stock: trilhos e vagões

roads fell to pieces: estradas se deterioraram

national television broadcasts: transmissões da televisão nacional

Produce Marketing Board: conselho de comercialização de produtos agrícolas

farms; when the governor of the central bank complained about **fiscal profligacy** in 1980, he was **thrown to his death from the roof of the central bank offices**. Stevens and his successor, Joseph Momoh, created monopolies, **expropriated assets**, and **looted diamond wealth**. In 1991 the regime **collapsed into a civil war**. Today most of Sierra Leone is controlled by 149 chiefs who are elected for life from "ruling houses." People without connections to those chiefs and ruling houses can quickly find their land expropriated. Sierra Leone's **per capita income** is far below what it was fifty years ago; it also has one of the worst **life-expectancy rates** in the world.

The economic backwardness of Africa made it vulnerable to colonialism, which replaced one form of absolutism with another.

Sub-Saharan Africa's poverty has emerged over a long period of time. But its origins and persistence **have nothing to do with** geography.

Many Africans are struggling to change their situation, aspiring to be wealthy and **live long and rewarding lives**, as witnessed by the thousands who **risk life and limb** trying to gain access to Europe and a better future for themselves and their families. Should we help them? If so, what can we do? I think we should help them, for several reasons. **First**, many things we do affect Africa, even if unintentionally, so we are already involved. **Second, we cannot help but be influenced** by Africa's poverty, which **breeds discontent** and **false messiahs**, such as Osama Bin Laden, that can lead to problems for the United States. **Finally**, we feel distress and **moral outrage** at witnessing such suffering and destitution.

What can we do? First, let us be clear about **foreign aid**: foreign aid is not the cure, but neither is it the cause. Sierra Leone got little in the way of aid in the 1970s and 1980s when Stevens was **running the country into the ground**. Such aid can be **siphoned off by corrupt politicians**, giving them more resources to play with, but the roots of Africa's economic problems long predate foreign aid.

---

fiscal profligacy: desperdício de dinheiro público

thrown to his death from the roof of the central bank offices: morreu após ser jogado do telhado do banco central

expropriated assets: expropriou bens

looted diamond wealth: roubou a riqueza proveniente dos diamantes

collapsed into a civil war: desintegrou-se numa guerra civil

per capita income: renda per capita

life-expectancy rates: taxas de expectativa de vida

have nothing to do with: não têm nada a ver com

live long and rewarding lives: ter vidas longas e produtivas, recompensadoras

risk life and limb: arriscam a vida

first: (marcador de discurso de enumeração) primeiro, em primeiro lugar

second: (marcador de discurso de enumeração) em segundo lugar

we cannot help but be influenced: não há como não ser influenciado

breeds discontent: fomenta a infelicidade

false messiahs: profetas falsos

finally: (marcador de discurso para concluir) finalmente, em conclusão

moral outrage: revolta (revoltado moralmente)

foreign aid: ajuda humanitária

running the country into the ground: quebrando o país, levando-o à falência

siphoned off by corrupt politicians: desviado por políticos corruptos

Three things would help sub-Saharan African societies **get on the right track economically**. First, give Africans more economic opportunities, which doesn't mean throwing money at them. What it does mean is opening markets to African exports and trade. In the seventeenth century, British trade was crucial for developing and strengthening those individuals who ultimately changed politics and property rights. This can also happen in Africa.

Second, economics must **play a bigger role** in foreign policy. Foreign policy toward Africa has been driven too much by short-term politics without focusing on economic development, but promoting prosperity in Africa is good long run foreign policy. Supporting dictators who are **"pro-Western"** risks creating an **"anti-Western"** society.

Finally, **development assistance** must help change the political trajectories of societies. By this I don't mean imposing democracy, though this could be good if the new democracy could be made to work. The historical evidence suggests that good political and economic institutions emerge from a **balance of power** in society. To achieve this, we should help **civil society** and the media **promote de facto checks and balances on rulers**. This is likely to be much more effective in Africa than promoting what James Madison, **principal crafter** of the U.S. Constitution, referred to as **"parchment" institutions**: those that exist on paper but aren't reflected in the interests and goals of the people.

JAMES ROBINSON
http://www.hoover.org

De acordo com o Programa das Nações Unidas para o Desenvolvimento (PNUD), o direito de propriedade formal continua bastante inseguro em muitos países do mundo. Economistas consideram a informalidade da posse um fator que contribui diretamente para a marginalização econômica da população, o uso insustentável de recursos naturais e a instabilidade política.

Questions

1. In the first paragraph, the expression "burning intellectual and policy issues" refers to the act of eliminating these issues. (C) (E)

2. According to a projection cited in the article, the number of poor people in Africa by 2015 will be over:
   a) 450 million
   b) 800 million
   c) 1 billion
   d) 400 million

3. On line 20, the word "plagued" could be replaced correctly by:
   a) sickened
   b) burdened
   c) contradicted
   d) benefitted

4. The word "whereas" on line 51 can be best translated as:
   a) contudo
   b) entretanto
   c) enquanto
   d) portanto

5. The average income of an American citizen is about 100 times that of an Ethiopian. (C) (E)

6. The Ethiopian King of Aksum was an early convert to Christianity. (C) (E)

7. In the 15th century, London was smaller than the capital of the Kongo, Mbanza. (C) (E)

8. In the paragraph that begins on line 314, the author makes the point that:
   a) foreign aid will end poverty in Africa
   b) foreign aid resources are always used responsibly by African governments
   c) African poverty started with foreign aid from western countries
   d) foreign aid is not going to solve Africa's poverty problems

9. In the excerpt below, the word "this" refers to "balance of power". (C) (E)

   The historical evidence suggests that good political and economic institutions emerge from a balance of power in society. To achieve **this**, *we should help civil society and the media promote de facto checks and balances on rulers.*

10 The main purpose of the article is to suggest a correlation between poverty and property rights. (C) (E)

Haiti: instituições e desenvolvimento

Patrick Emerson é professor de economia na Universidade Estadual de Oregon. Neste artigo, ele apresenta alguns pensamentos sobre as instituições haitianas.

Haiti: institutions and development

1 Why is Haiti so poor? Tyler Cowan lists some possible reasons and there are many other essays **floating around in the blogosphere**. They all have a common component: **governance issues**. Haiti
5 is a **former French colony**, was occupied by the US, has had **malevolent dictators** and is **rife with corruption**. In economics, such issues **fall under the general rubric** of "institutions". Institutions refers to a nation's laws and legal system that
10 protect individual and **private property rights** that promote **private investment**, and government and bureaucracies that provide infrastructure, education, regulation, etc. All of this is thought to be critical to development and most **poorly**
15 **performing economies** can be described as having **weak institutions**.

Though it **makes a lot of intuitive sense**, it is a very hard thing to isolate in an empirical study. The problem, of course is that institutions and
20 **growth** are very **highly correlated**, but is it good economic performance that accounts for the **strong institutions** or is it the strong institutions that created the preconditions for the strong growth?

institutions and development: instituições e desenvolvimento
floating around in the blogosphere: circulando na Internet
governance issues: questões sobre governança
former French colony: ex-colônia francesa
malevolent dictators: ditadores maldosos, malevolentes
rife with corruption: com alto índice de corrupção, altamente corrupto
fall under the general rubric: se encaixam na categoria geral
private property rights: direitos de propriedade
private investment: investimentos privados
poorly performing economies: economias com baixo desempenho
weak institutions: instituições fracas
makes a lot of intuitive sense: faz sentido intuitivamente
growth: crescimento econômico
highly correlated: altamente correlacionados, interligados
strong institutions: instituições

It is yet another case of **correlation vs. causation**. In order to try and identify the **causal link** between institutions and development, you need to find a variable that helps explain the institutional quality of a country but is not correlated with the unexplained variation in growth. This is hard to do.

Three economists, Daron Acemoglu, Simon Johnson and James Robinson, wrote a **seminal paper** a few years back that did exactly this. They used **settler mortality data** to identify countries that were more and less **hospitable to european settlement** during the beginning of the colonial era. The idea is that in countries where settler mortality was relatively low, colonizers were more likely to **set up more long term or more permanent institutions** (England in the US, Australia and India for example), in countries with high settler mortality rates the incentives were to set up a **minimal institutional architecture**, **extract resources**, and get out (Belgium in the Congo and more generally tropical countries had more diseases). Of course the story doesn't work if the mortality rates are the same in the local populations, but in general those populations had become resistant to the local diseases and it was mainly the Europeans that were **susceptible to these illnesses**. They use this **disease climate variable** as a determinant of the development of good institutions (while controlling for many other observable [factors], like for instance, the nationality of the colonizer) and argue fairly convincingly that this settler mortality is unrelated to the unexplained variation in subsequent **growth rates**. **Their findings are robust**: good institutions are important for good development.

So where does Haiti stand in this study? Its settler mortality was in the middle and fairly average for the Caribbean, but it was colonized by France and there is some evidence that this is worse than being colonized by England or Spain as were other more successful Caribbean economies. But the **kleptocratic**

Duvalier reign in Haiti was probably the most damaging aspect of Haiti's 20th Century growth.

Patrick Emerson
http://oregonecon.blogspot.com

kleptocratic Duvalier reign: o governo corrupto de Duvalier. Cleptocracia refere-se a um regime político-social em que predominam as práticas corruptas.

"No Haiti, a nação mais pobre da América Latina, o total de ativos dos pobres é mais de cento e cinquenta vezes maior do que todo o investimento estrangeiro recebido desde a independência do Haiti da França em 1804. [...] Entretanto, os cidadãos detêm esses recursos de forma defeituosa: casas construídas em terras cujos direitos de propriedade não estão adequadamente registrados, empresas não constituídas em sociedade, indústrias localizadas onde investidores não podem vê-las. Porque os direitos a esses bens não são adequadamente documentados, esses ativos não podem ser facilmente transformados em capital, não podem ser trocados fora dos estreitos círculos locais onde as pessoas se conhecem e confiam uns nos outros, não podem ser utilizados como garantia para um empréstimo e não podem ser usados como um investimento. Em países desenvolvidos, pelo contrário, cada parcela de terra, cada prédio, cada peça de equipamento ou estoque é representado por um documento de propriedade que é o sinal visível de um vasto processo oculto que conecta todos esses ativos para o resto da economia. Graças a esse processo de representação, os ativos podem levar uma vida invisível, paralela à sua existência material. [...] Por este processo o Ocidente injeta vida em ativos e os fazem gerar capital."
Hernando de Soto (economista peruano)

Texto adaptado do livro *The Mystery of Capital*.

http://www.ild.org.pe/index.php?option=com_content&view=article&id=184&Itemid=409&lang=en

Questions

1 In the first paragraph, the expression "floating around" could be replaced by "being distributed". (C) (E)

2 The word "they" (line 3) refers to "essays". (C) (E)

3 The word "growth", as it appears in the context of the article, refers to:
   a) economic growth
   b) physical growth
   c) growth of pathogens that cause disease
   d) population growth

4 The concept of "correlation" mentioned in line 24 refers to:
   a) a relation of causality
   b) the relationship between two variables which does not imply causality
   c) a confirmation of dependency
   d) a random relation between variables

5 Although it can be complex and sometimes difficult to determine with absolute certainty, "causality" is defined as the relationship between two events, where the second event is a consequence of the first. (C) (E)

6 On line 54, the expression "for instance" could be replaced by "by example". (C) (E)

7 In the last paragraph, the autor's use of the word "reign" implies that he considers that president Duvalier governed like a king in Haiti. (C) (E)

8 The main point of the article is to suggest a causal link between:
   a) settler mortality and disease
   b) European intitutions and corruption
   c) climate and successful settlement
   d) economic performance and institutions

10

A economia dos impérios

No artigo a seguir, o economista Krassimir Petrov argumenta que a hegemonia dos Estados Unidos da América desde os acordos de Bretton Woods (1944) é baseada fundamentalmente na manutenção do dólar como a principal moeda internacional. O economista demonstra que a posição hegemônica do dólar habilita os Estados Unidos a "tributar" outros países indiretamente por intermédio da inflação. A manutenção do dólar como moeda hegemônica, de acordo com os argumentos de Petrov, seria um dos sustentáculos do "império americano" e, portanto, o principal motivo por trás das intervenções militares e da diplomacia daquele país.

The economics of empires

A **nation-state taxes** its own citizens, while an empire **taxes** other nation-states. The history of empires, from Greek and Roman, to Ottoman and British, teaches that the economic foundation of every single empire is the taxation of other nations. The imperial ability to tax has always rested on a better and stronger economy, and as a consequence, a better and stronger military. One part of the **subjects' taxes** went to **improve the living standards** of the empire; the other part went to strengthen the military dominance necessary to enforce the collection of those taxes.

Historically, taxing the subject state has been in various forms — usually gold and silver, where those were considered money, but also slaves, soldiers, crops, cattle, or other agricultural and natural resources, whatever economic goods the empire demanded and the subject-state could deliver. Historically, imperial taxation has always been direct: the subject state **handed over** the economic goods directly to the empire.

nation-state: Estado-nação, Estado
taxes: tributa, cobra impostos

subjects' taxes: os impostos extraídos dos súditos
improve the living standards: melhorar a qualidade de vida

handed over: entregava

For the first time in history, in the twentieth century, America was able to tax the world indirectly, **through inflation**. It did not enforce the direct payment of taxes like all of its predecessor empires did, but distributed instead its own **fiat currency**, the U.S. Dollar, to other nations in exchange for **goods** with the intended consequence of inflating and devaluing those dollars and paying back later each dollar with less economic goods — the difference capturing the **U.S. imperial tax**. Here is how this happened.

Early in the 20th century, the U.S. economy began to dominate the world economy. The U.S. dollar was **tied to gold**, so that the value of the dollar neither increased, nor decreased, but remained the same amount of gold. **The Great Depression**, with its **preceding inflation** from 1921 to 1929 and its subsequent **ballooning government deficits**, had substantially increased the amount of currency in circulation, and thus rendered the **backing of U.S. dollars by gold** impossible. This led **Roosevelt** to **decouple** the dollar from gold in 1932. **Up to this point**, the U.S. may have well dominated the world economy, but from an economic point of view, it was not an empire. The fixed value of the dollar did not allow the Americans to extract economic benefits from other countries by supplying them with dollars convertible to gold.

Economically, the American Empire was born with **Bretton Woods** in 1945. The U.S. dollar was not fully convertible to gold, but was made convertible to gold only to foreign governments. This established the dollar as the **reserve currency** of the world. It was possible, because during **WWII**, the United States had supplied its allies with provisions, demanding gold as payment, thus accumulating a significant portion of the world's gold. An Empire would not have been possible if, following the Bretton Woods arrangement, the dollar supply was kept limited and within the availability of gold, so as to fully exchange back dollars for gold. However, the **guns-and-butter policy** of the 1960's was an imperial one: **the dollar**

supply was relentlessly increased to finance [the war in] Vietnam and **LBJ**'s Great Society. Most of those dollars were handed over to foreigners in exchange for **economic goods**, without the prospect of **buying them back** at the same value. The increase in **dollar holdings** of foreigners via persistent U.S. trade deficits was **tantamount to a tax** — the classical **inflation tax** that a country imposes on its own citizens, this time around an inflation tax that the U.S. imposed on rest of the world.

When in 1970-1971 foreigners demanded payment for their dollars in gold, the U.S. Government **defaulted on its payment** on August 15, 1971. While the popular **spin** told the story of "severing the link between the dollar and gold", in reality the denial to pay back in gold was an **act of bankruptcy** by the U.S. Government. Essentially, the U.S. declared itself an Empire. It had extracted an enormous amount of economic goods from the rest of the world, with no intention or ability to return those goods, and the world was powerless to respond — the world was taxed and it could not do anything about it.

From that point on, to sustain the American Empire and to continue to tax the rest of the world, the United States had to force the world to continue to accept **ever-depreciating dollars** in exchange for economic goods and to have the world hold more and more of those depreciating dollars. It had to give the world an economic reason to hold them, and that reason was **oil**.

In 1971, as it became clearer and clearer that the U.S Government would not be able to buy back its dollars in gold, it made in 1972-73 an **iron-clad arrangement** with Saudi Arabia to support the power of the House of Saud in exchange for accepting only U.S. dollars for its oil. The rest of **OPEC** was to **follow suit** and also accept only dollars. Because the world had to buy oil from the Arab oil countries, it had the reason to hold dollars as payment for oil. Because the world needed ever increasing quantities of oil at ever increasing oil prices, the world's demand for dollars could only increase. Even though

the dollar supply was relentlessly increased: a quantidade de dólares impressos foi cada vez mais expandido
LBJ: presidente Lyndon Baines Johnson
economic goods: bens de consumo
buying them back: comprando-os de volta
dollar holdings: reservas em dólar
tantamount to a tax: efetivamente um imposto
inflation tax: um "imposto inflacionário"

defaulted on its payment: deu calote na dívida
spin: informações enganosas e manipuladas
act of bankruptcy: um ato de falência

ever-depreciating dollars: dólares cada vez mais depreciados

oil: petróleo

iron-clad arrangement: um acordo sólido, que não poderia ser quebrado
OPEC: abreviação de "Organization of the Petroleum Exporting Countries", Organização dos Países Exportadores de Petróleo (OPEP)
follow suit: seguir o exemplo

dollars could no longer be exchanged for gold, they were now exchangeable for oil.

The economic essence of this arrangement was that the dollar was now **backed by oil**. As long as that was the case, the world had to accumulate increasing amounts of dollars, because they needed those dollars to buy oil. As long as the dollar was the only acceptable payment for oil, its dominance in the world was assured, and the American Empire could continue to tax the rest of the world. If, for any reason, the dollar lost its oil backing, the American Empire **would cease to exist**. **Thus**, Imperial survival dictated that oil be sold only for dollars. It also dictated that oil reserves were spread around various sovereign states that weren't strong enough, politically or militarily, to demand payment for oil in something else. If someone demanded a different payment, he had to be convinced, either by political pressure or military means, to **change his mind**.

The man that actually did demand Euros for his oil was Saddam Hussein in 2000. At first, his demand was **met with ridicule**, later with neglect, but as it became clearer that he **meant business**, political pressure was exerted to change his mind. When other countries, like Iran, wanted payment in other currencies, most notably Euro and Yen, the danger to the dollar was **clear and present**, and a **punitive action was in order**. Bush's **Shock-and-Awe** in Iraq was not about Saddam's nuclear capabilities, about defending human rights, about spreading democracy, or even about seizing oil fields; it was about defending the dollar, **ergo** the American Empire. It was about **setting an example** that anyone who demanded payment in currencies other than U.S. Dollars would be likewise punished.

Many have criticized Bush for **staging the war** in Iraq in order to seize Iraqi oil fields. **However**, those critics can't explain why Bush would want to seize those fields — he could simply print dollars for nothing and use them to get all the oil in the world that he needs. He must have had some other reason to invade Iraq.

---

backed by oil: garantia de conversibilidade por petróleo

would cease to exist: desapareceria
thus: (marcador de discurso de conclusão) logo, portanto, então, por isso, por conseguinte, por isto, assim

change his mind: mudar de ideia

met with ridicule: ridicularizado
meant business: estava sério

clear and present: óbvio e iminente, claro e real
punitive action was in order: uma ação punitiva era necessária
Shock-and-Awe: ações bélicas de grande força destrutiva visando causar efeitos psicológicos
ergo: portanto
setting an example: dando um exemplo

staging the war: iniciar a guerra
however: (marcador de discurso para contrastar) entretanto

History teaches that an empire should go to war for one of two reasons: (1) to defend itself or (2) benefit from war; if not, as Paul Kennedy illustrates in his magisterial *The Rise and Fall of the Great Powers*, a **military overstretch will drain its economic resources** and precipitate its collapse. **Economically speaking**, in order for an empire to initiate and conduct a war, **its benefits must outweigh its military and social costs**. Benefits from Iraqi **oil fields** are **hardly worth** the long-term, multi-year military cost. Instead, Bush must have gone into Iraq to defend his Empire. **Indeed**, this is the case: two months after the United States invaded Iraq, the **Oil for Food Program** was terminated, the Iraqi Euro accounts **were switched back** to dollars, and oil was sold once again only for U.S. dollars. No longer could the world buy oil from Iraq with Euros. Global dollar supremacy was once again restored. Bush descended victoriously from a fighter jet and declared the **mission accomplished** — he had successfully defended the U.S. dollar, and thus the American Empire.

KRASSIMIR PETROV
http://www.energybulletin.net/

military overstretch: engajamento militar excessivo
will drain its economic resources: acabará com seus recursos econômicos
economically speaking: em relação à economia
its benefits must outweigh its military and social costs: seus benefícios terão de compensar os custos militares e sociais
oil fields: campos petrolíferos
hardly worth: mal compensam
indeed: (marcador de discurso para enfatizar antes de afirmar algo) de fato
Oil for Food Program: programa da Organização das Nações Unidas que permitiria que o Iraque vendesse petróleo no mercado mundial em troca de comida, remédios e outros suprimentos de valor humanitário.
were switched back: foram revertidos
mission accomplished: missão cumprida

De acordo com dados oficiais do Departamento de Defesa, havia 865 bases militares norte-americanas em cerca de 130 países em 2009 (existem 196 países no mundo, incluindo o mais novo país, Sudão do Sul). O analista militar Chalmers Johnson estima que hoje existem mais de mil bases militares norte-americanas. Especialista em política internacional, Johnson escreveu vários livros, incluindo três análises das consequências do "Império Americano": *Blowback: The Costs and Consequences of American Empire*, *The Sorrows of Empire: Militarism, Secrecy, and the End of the Republic* e *Nemesis: The Last Days of the American Republic*.

Questions

1 According to the article, the United States enjoys a unique historical

situation insofar as being able to tax other countries indirectly. This ability is a consequence of:
a) the American supremacy in military power
b) the dollar being the world's reserve currency and the fact that all oil purchases are made in dollars
c) the lack of other alternatives available
d) universal preference for the US currency

2 The author argues in paragraph 9 that the most important reason for the American invasion of Iraq during the first Gulf War was:
a) the presence of weapons of mass destruction in Iraq
b) the personal animosity between Bush and Hussein
c) Iraq's lack of compliance with Bretton Woods
d) Saddam Hussein's intention to break the dollar monopoly in the oil market

3 The Unites States government abandoned the gold standard for the dollar in:
a) 1932
b) 1921 to 1929
c) 1945
d) 1971

4 According to the paragraph that begins on line 94, which of the following was not a consequence of the agreement between the US government and Saudi Arabia in 1972-1973:
a) the US could buy back its dollars held by other nations
b) the US dollar became effectively convertible to oil
c) countries were forced to hold US dollars so they could purchase oil
d) the demand for US dollars increased
e) all OPEC nations adopted the US dollar as the medium of exchange for oil

5 According to the arguments in the text, judge the following items:
a) the US "imperial tax" (line 31) refers to a tax that all countries pay directly to the US government (C) (E)
b) the author defines empires by their ability to tax other nation-states (C) (E)
c) the reference to "guns-and-butter" (line 62) is associated with the Johnson administration. (C) (E)
d) the concept of "inflation tax" mentioned in line 71 refers to a subtle transfer of wealth from individuals to the government (C) (E)
e) the American Empire rests upon the hegemony of the US currency (C) (E)

11

A política de repressão aos entorpecentes

Neste breve artigo, o jornalista Ed Brayton relata a admissão feita pelo mais alto oficial norte-americano encarregado de formular políticas de controle de drogas ilícitas: a política tradicional de repressão "não tem sido um sucesso". A chamada "guerra contra as drogas" foi instituída há 40 anos pelo presidente Richard Nixon. Desde então, a despeito do gasto trilionário, o uso de entorpecentes e a criminalidade aumentaram substancialmente naquele país. De acordo com Jeffrey Miron, economista da Universidade de Harvard, o governo gasta US$ 44 bilhões por ano para reprimir e para encarcerar meio milhão de pessoas acusadas de crimes relacionados a entorpecentes. Devido aos gastos e ao fracasso dos objetivos, o atual paradigma repressivo tem sido amplamente debatido e questionado na sociedade norte-americana, inclusive por juízes e associações de policiais.

Drug czar admits war on drugs failure

1 The head of the Office of National Drug Control Policy has admitted that the war on drugs is a failure. After 40 years, the United States' war on drugs has cost $1 trillion and hundreds of thousands of lives, and
5 for what? Drug use is rampant and violence even more brutal and widespread. Even U.S. **drug czar** Gil Kerlikowske concedes the strategy hasn't worked.

 "**In the grand scheme**, it has not been successful," Kerlikowske told The Associated Press.
10 "Forty years later, the concern about drugs and drug problems is, if anything, magnified, intensified."

 If anything, he **understates** it. It isn't just that the war on drugs has failed; it's that the war on drugs creates many, if not most, of the very problems
15 used to justify the war in the first place.

drug czar: oficial do governo responsável pela elaboração e gerenciamento das políticas contra o tráfico de drogas ilícitas nos Estados Unidos

war on drugs: política norte-americana de controle das drogas via repressão policial e ações militares em outros países

in the grand scheme: em geral, numa perspectiva ampla

understates: subestima

The zealous **drug warriors** justify the war by pointing out the existence of violent gangs that run drugs — but those drug gangs only exist because drugs are illegal. You don't see violent turf wars
20 between Stolichnaya and Skyy*, or between Miller and Budweiser** because they compete the way all legitimate corporations do.

They justify the war on drugs by pointing to the amount of crime that takes place by those who are
25 addicted and need the money to buy drugs. But **prohibition artificially inflates the price** and only makes that crime **more common than it otherwise would be**.

Drug use should be treated just like alcohol use —
30 regulated, taxed and restricted to adults. Drug abuse should be treated like alcohol abuse — as a **public health problem**, not as a criminal problem. It's time to declare defeat and **bring the troops home**.

ED BRAYTON
http://scienceblogs.com

drug warriors: pessoas que sustentam a atual política

* marcas de vodca
** marcas de cerveja

prohibition artificially inflates the price: a proibição causa o aumento de preço artificialmente
more common than it otherwise would be: mais comum do que seria normalmente
public health problem: uma questão de saúde pública
bring the troops home: tirar as tropas do campo

Bellona, personagem mitológica e esposa do deus da guerra romano, Marte, é a raiz etimológica de várias palavras importantes em inglês relacionadas à guerra. Por exemplo, *antebellum* (antes da guerra) é uma palavra comum para se referir ao período que precedeu da Guerra Civil Americana (1861-1865). *Bellicose* (belicoso, agressivo), *belligerent* (beligerante, agressivo), *rebellion* (rebelião) também são palavras derivadas da mesma raiz.

Questions

1 According to the author, the estimated total costs of the "war on drugs" are:
   a) one million dollars and thousands of lives
   b) one billion dollars and hundreds of thousands of lives
   c) justified by the efficacy of the program
   d) one trillion dollars and hundreds of thousands of lives

2. The word "widespread" in the sentence "drug use is rampant and violence even more brutal and widespread" (line 6) means:
   a) common
   b) specific
   c) concentrated
   d) cruel
   e) large

3. At the beginning of the second paragraph, the words "in the grand scheme" could be correctly replaced by "overall". (C) (E)

4. On line 21 the word "they" refers to "gangs". (C) (E)

5. According to the author, the "war on drugs" can be associated with all of the following, except:
   a) higher crime rates
   b) a reduction in drug use
   c) higher prices for those drugs
   d) deaths of human beings
   e) violence in the US

6. Read the sentence below and judge the following statements.

   *But prohibition artificially inflates the price and only makes **that** crime more common than it otherwise would be.*

   a) From the sentence above, we could logically infer that the decriminalization of drugs would lead to a drop in crime. (C) (E)
   b) In the sentence above, the word "that" is referring to a specific crime cited earlier. (C) (E)

12

WikiLeaks

WikiLeaks é uma organização sem fins lucrativos sediada na Suécia que publica informações confidenciais de governos. Ao longo de 2010, a organização publicou grande volume de documentos confidenciais do governo dos Estados Unidos, com forte repercussão internacional. Em fevereiro de 2011, o WikiLeaks foi indicado ao Prêmio Nobel da Paz por um parlamentar norueguês. O autor da proposta disse que o trabalho dessa organização constitui "uma das contribuições mais importantes para a liberdade de expressão e transparência" no século XXI. O artigo abaixo, sobre a importância de uma imprensa desafiadora, encontra-se no site da organização.

Why the media is important

Publishing improves transparency, and this transparency creates a better society for all people. Better scrutiny leads to reduced corruption and stronger democracies in all society's institutions, including government, corporations and other organisations. A healthy, vibrant and inquisitive journalistic media **plays a vital role** in achieving these goals. We are part of that media.

Scrutiny requires information. Historically, information has been costly in terms of human life, **human rights** and economics. As a result of technical advances, particularly the internet and **cryptography** — the risks of conveying important information can be lowered. In its **landmark ruling** on the Pentagon Papers, the **US Supreme Court** ruled that "only a **free and unrestrained press** can effectively expose deception in government." We agree.

We believe that it is not only the people of one country that keep their own government honest, but also the people of other countries who are **watching** that government through the media.

plays a vital role: desempenha uma função fundamental

human rights: direitos humanos

cryptography: criptografia, tecnologia de proteção de dados

landmark ruling: uma decisão jurídica importante

US Supreme Court: supremo tribunal federal norte-americano

free and unrestrained press: imprensa livre e sem restrições

watching: vigiando

In the years **leading up to** the founding of **WikiLeaks**, we observed the world's publishing media becoming less independent and far less willing to **ask the hard questions** of government, corporations and other institutions. We believed this needed to change.

WikiLeaks has provided a new model of journalism. Because we are not motivated by **making a profit**, we work cooperatively with other publishing and media organisations **around the globe**, instead of following the traditional model of competing with other media. We don't **hoard our information**; we make the original documents available with our news stories. Readers can verify the truth of what we have reported themselves. Like a **wire service**, WikiLeaks reports stories that are often picked up by other media outlets. We encourage this. We believe the world's media should work together as much as possible to bring stories to a **broad international readership**.

The great American president Thomas Jefferson once observed that **the price of freedom is eternal vigilance**. We believe the journalistic media **plays a key role** in this vigilance.

Principled leaking has **changed the course of history for the better**. It can alter the course of history in the present, and it can lead us to a better future.

Consider Daniel Ellsberg, working within the US government during the Vietnam War. He comes into contact with the Pentagon Papers, a **meticulously kept record** of military and strategic planning throughout the war. Those papers **reveal the depths to which the US government has sunk** in deceiving the American people about the war.

Yet the public and the media know nothing of this urgent and shocking information. **Indeed**, **secrecy laws** are being used to keep the public ignorant of **gross dishonesty** practised by their own government. **In spite of** those secrecy laws and at great personal risk, Ellsberg manages to disseminate the Pentagon papers to journalists and to the world.

---

leading up to: que precederam
WikiLeaks: organização sem fins lucrativos responsável pela divulgação de documentos. O nome "wiki" refere-se a uma tecnologia aberta para criar sites colaborativos na Internet, e "leaks" refere-se a divulgações sem permissão oficial.
ask the hard questions: fazer perguntas difíceis, desafiar
making a profit: ganhar dinheiro, lucrar
around the globe: ao redor do mundo, internacionalmente
hoard our information: seguramos nossas informações
wire service: distribuidora de notícias
broad international readership: amplo público leitor internacional
the price of freedom is eternal vigilance: o preço da liberdade é a vigilância eterna
plays a key role: desempenha um papel chave
principled leaking: divulgação responsável (a partir de princípios morais)
changed the course of history for the better: mudou o rumo da história para melhor
meticulously kept record: relatórios detalhadamente elaborados
reveal the depths to which the US government has sunk: revelam o baixo nível ao qual o governo norte-americano chegou
indeed: (marcador de discurso para enfatizar antes de afirmar algo) de fato
secrecy laws: leis de sigilo
gross dishonesty: grande desonestidade
in spite of: apesar de, a despeito de

Despite criminal charges against Ellsberg, **eventually dropped**, the release of the Pentagon Papers shocks the world, exposes the government lying and helps to shorten the war and save thousands of both American and Vietnamese lives.

The power of principled leaking **to call governments, corporations and institutions to account** is amply demonstrated through recent history. The **public scrutiny** of otherwise unaccountable and secretive institutions forces them to consider the ethical implications of their actions. Which official will **chance** a secret, corrupt transaction when the public is likely to **find out**? What repressive plan will be **carried out** when it is revealed to the **citizenry**, not just of its own country, but the world? When the risks of embarrassment and discovery increase, **the tables are turned** against conspiracy, corruption, exploitation and oppression.

Open government answers injustice rather than causing it. Open government exposes and undoes corruption. Open governance is the most effective method of promoting good governance.

Today, with authoritarian governments in power in much of the world, increasing authoritarian tendencies in democratic governments, and increasing amounts of power vested in unaccountable corporations, the need for openness and transparency is **greater than ever**.

WikiLeaks' interest is the revelation of the truth. Unlike the covert activities of **state intelligence agencies**, as a media publisher WikiLeaks relies upon the power of overt fact to enable and **empower citizens** to bring feared and corrupt governments and corporations to justice.

With its anonymous **drop box**, WikiLeaks provides **an avenue** for every government official, every bureaucrat, and every corporate worker, who **becomes privy** to **damning information** that their institution wants to hide but the public needs to know. What conscience cannot contain, and institutional secrecy unjustly conceals, WikiLeaks can **broadcast** to the world. **It is telling that**

---

despite: a despeito de, apesar de
criminal charges: acusações criminais
eventually dropped: no final descartadas

to call governments, corporations and institutions to account: exigir prestação de contas ("accountability") dos governos, corporações e instituições
public scrutiny: escrutínio público, examinação pública

chance: arriscar
find out: descobrir
carried out: executado
citizenry: conjunto de cidadãos, público

the tables are turned: as condições se invertem

greater than ever: maior do que nunca
state intelligence agencies: órgãos de inteligência estatais

empower citizens: capacitar os cidadãos, empoderar

drop box: "caixa" onde se pode deixar documentos ou informações
an avenue: um meio

becomes privy: fique sabendo, tenha acesso
damning information: informações que comprometem
broadcast: divulgar
it is telling that: é particularmente interessante (ou relevante) que

a number of government agencies in different countries (and indeed some entire countries) have tried to **ban access** to WikiLeaks. This is of course a silly response, akin to the ostrich burying its head in the sand. A far better response would be to behave in more ethical ways.

ban access: proibir o acesso

Authoritarian governments, oppressive institutions and corrupt corporations should be subject to the pressure, not merely of international diplomacy, **freedom of information laws** or even periodic elections, but of something far stronger — the consciences of the people within them.

freedom of information laws: leis que garantem acesso à informação

www.wikileaks.org

A palavra "wiki" refere-se a uma tecnologia aberta para criar sites colaborativos na Internet. Originalmente, a palavra vem da língua ancestral havaiana e significa "rápido". "Leaks" (vazamentos) refere-se a divulgações sem permissão oficial.

Questions

1. According to the article, all of the following are benefits of independent journalism, except:
   a) improved transparency
   b) reduced corruption
   c) better social control
   d) stronger democracy
   e) better accountability

2. In the excerpt below, the word "watching" could be correctly replaced by "seeing". (C) (E)

   *We believe that it is not only the people of one country that keep their own government honest, but also the people of other countries who are **watching** that government through the media.*

3. In the excerpt below, the word "it" refers to "the course of history". (C) (E)

Principled leaking has changed the course of history for the better. **It** *can alter the course of history in the present, and it can lead us to a better future.*

4 In paragraph 9, the author argues that legal measures are increasingly instituted to improve transparency in government. (C) (E)

5 The words "in spite of" in the excerpt below can be correctly replaced by "despite". (C) (E)

In spite of *those secrecy laws and at great personal risk, Ellsberg manages to disseminate the Pentagon papers to journalists and to the world.*

6 Judge the following items.
   a) The expression "to call to account" (line 69) can be defined as demanding that actions must be listed and justified. (C) (E)
   b) The word "chance" in line 75 could be replaced by "opportunity". (C) (E)
   c) The expression "to ask the hard questions" (line 25) could be replaced by "to challenge". (C) (E)

7 In the excerpt below, the word "this" refers to "ban access". (C) (E)

It is telling that a number of government agencies in different countries (and indeed some entire countries) have tried to ban access to WikiLeaks. **This** *is of course a silly response, akin to the ostrich burying its head in the sand.*

8 The main point of the article is:
   a) A strong and independent media is fundamental to maintain good governance and create a better society.
   b) Governments dislike media challenges and should make confidential most of their work.
   c) All governments are corrupt and need strong media scrutiny.
   d) Good governance comes from being able to control and direct the media.
   e) The leaks by Daniel Ellsberg helped end the Vietnam War.

9 In the text, the author cites at least two governmental sources to support his main argument. (C) (E)

13

A Revolução do Jasmim na Tunísia

Pela primeira vez na história, líderes de países árabes foram depostos em decorrência de sublevações populares. Os protestos começaram na Tunísia, país mulçumano localizado ao norte da África, e se alastraram para o Egito, Líbia, Baréin, Irã, Síria e Iêmen. Trata-se de um movimento popular, provavelmente de grandes consequências históricas, que pode ser comparado à queda do Muro de Berlim, em 1989, e à Primavera dos Povos de 1848.

The Jasmine Revolution

1 Analysts and experts never cease to analyze the sociopolitical nature of the Arab world. Especially since **9/11**, most have **set their expectations low** and [have] been cynical about any social or political
5 change taking place in the land of **strongmen** and dictatorial power. We, **Middle Easterners**, have been accused of being passive, unable to mobilize, and **unwilling to fight for our rights**.
    After blowing all over the globe, the long-
10 **awaited winds of political change have decided to finally visit the Middle East.** North African countries have in the past few years seen a large number of riots, **sit-ins**, strikes and demonstrations to protest **low wages** and a **high cost of living**, but
15 a ruthless police state has always stopped these **outcries** of anger and frustration from developing into a popular revolution **ousting a regime from power**. Tunisia's Jasmine revolution on January 14 marked the first successful attempt to **overthrow a**
20 **dictator** by a popular revolution. And it took place

the Jasmine Revolution: revolta popular na Tunísia, em janeiro de 2011, que levou à expulsão do ditador daquele país
9/11: a data 11 de setembro de 2001, quando aconteceram os ataques terroristas nos EUA
set their expectations low: têm baixas expectativas
strongmen: líderes autoritários
Middle Easterners: povo do Oriente Médio
unwilling to fight for our rights: indispostos a lutar pelos nossos direitos
after blowing all over the globe, the long-awaited winds of political change have decided to finally visit the Middle East: após espalharem-se pelo mundo, as tão esperadas mudanças políticas finalmente chegaram ao Oriente Médio
sit-ins: protestos pacíficos com a ocupação de um local
low wages: salários baixos
high cost of living: alto custo de vida

in a country that was thought to be one of the most stable in a region where autocracy was believed to be **deep-rooted** and nearly impossible to abolish.

The people of Tunisia proved us all wrong by forcing dictator Zine el-Abidine Ben Ali out in a way unprecedented in the Arab world. The only way an Arab dictator would take his suitcase and escape his own country used to be through a **military coup**, until a few days ago, thanks to the people of Tunisia.

But what does that mean to neighboring countries like Morocco, Algeria, Libya and Egypt? No one can claim it will have no impact, because it already has. At least four people have **self-immolated** in Egypt out of desperation, which is how it all started in Tunisia when Mohamed Bouazizi **burnt himself to death sparking non-stop riots** for three weeks that protested **deteriorating living conditions** and **high unemployment**. Riots have erupted in Yemen, Jordan, Morocco, Egypt and Algeria since Tunisia's **uprising**.

Democracy, like authoritarianism, is contagious. It is hard to find a **standalone** democracy surrounded by dictatorships, or vice versa. In the **Autumn of Nations** in 1989, a few Eastern European countries overthrew their communist regimes, which **led to the collapse** of the Soviet Union and the collapse of many communist regimes in the region after that. Communism was not hurt just in Eastern Europe, but in many countries all over the world following the Soviet Union collapse. Another major **ripple effect** was Latin America's serious steps towards democracy over the past three decades in a fashion rarely seen in the developing world. If real democracy takes hold in Tunisia, it will increase the chances of it happening elsewhere close by.

However, it's hard to predict the extent of the effect on neighboring countries because, **even though** they belong to the same region and share a lot in common, every country still has a different economic, social and political nature. **Copying and pasting** a Tunisian scenario in Egypt, Libya, Algeria or Morocco is unlikely to happen. However, North Africa now seems well prepared and more ready than ever to dispose of its authoritarian regimes and gradually start a new era of **people's empowerment** due to a steady increase of dissidence and a growing **political momentum** in some of these countries, in reaction to **dire economic situations**, high levels of corruption and **worsening human rights conditions**.

Even though Tunisia's revolution might not be replicated, it will still bring many benefits to the people of neighboring countries.

Firstly, it acts as a **clear warning message** to authoritarian regimes that **over-relying on security apparatuses** to remain in power with no popular support has proved unsustainable for authoritarian regimes. It also conveys the message that the economic and political rights of the masses must be **dealt with**, and cannot be silenced **by a heavy hand**.

Secondly, it ends the myth that Islamists are the only group capable of **toppling regimes** in this region — an idea established after the Iranian revolution and the assassination of Egyptian president Anwar Sadat in the late 1970s and the early 1980s, one that has been used by secular dictatorships in the North African region as a **scare tactic** to win the West's support. The idea is simple: imposed secular authoritarianism has been for long preferred over an elected Islamic regime by the world's superpowers. Former **U.S. Secretary of State** Condoleezza Rice once stated that the United States has long favored stability over democracy in the Middle East and ended up achieving **neither**.

It also implies that the way for a government to gain legitimacy is from its own people rather than by allying with **superpowers**, as they all **turned their backs** on Ben Ali after he was overthrown by his people. France, his biggest former ally, has refused to **grant him asylum**. Many regimes relied solely on their alliance with Western superpowers **at the expense of their own people**. This might no longer be **a good bargain** for Arab dictators.

Whether or not we will see the fall of one North African regime after the other is hard to predict and

105 not guaranteed, but the good news is that Tunisia's revolution will **spread the scent of its jasmine** to oppressed nations all over the region, inspiring and empowering people in their fight against unjust regimes.

OSAMA DIAB
http://www.worldpress.org/

> spread the scent of its jasmine: espalhar o perfume de jasmim (as mudanças sociais)

Por que "jasmim"? De acordo com o periódico inglês *The Independent*, um jornalista tunisiano foi o primeiro a usar o termo "Revolução do Jasmim". O jasmim é um dos símbolos da Tunísia e, de acordo com o jornalista, a cor branca simboliza a tolerância dos tunisianos e o aroma doce do arbusto é muito apreciado em seu país.

Questions

1 From the sentence that begins on line 11, it can be inferred that inflation is a problem in North Africa. (C) (E)

2 The word "unprecedented" in the sentence "The people of Tunisia proved us all wrong by forcing dictator Zine el-Abidine Ben Ali out in a way *unprecedented* in the Arab world" can be replaced by:
   a) not seen before
   b) occurring commonly
   c) rarely seen
   d) present
   e) impossible

3 With the sentence "Democracy, like authoritarianism, is contagious" the author means:
   a) authoritarianism is as common as democracy in the world
   b) authoritarianism can easily replace democracy
   c) democratic countries often appear in regions known for authoritarian regimes such as the Middle East
   d) the change to democracy in one country can often influence neighboring countries to change as well
   e) Eastern European democracy has spread to the Middle East

4 The word "that" in the sentence below refers to:

*In the Autumn of Nations in 1989, a few Eastern European countries overthrew their communist regimes, which led to the collapse of the Soviet Union and the collapse of many communist regimes in the region after **that**.*

   a) the Autumn of Nations in 1989
   b) the collapse of the Soviet Union
   c) communist regimes
   d) overthrow
   e) many communist regimes

5 The word "fashion" in the sentence "in a *fashion* rarely seen in the developing world" can be correctly replaced with:
   a) time
   b) way
   c) place
   d) organization
   e) velocity

6 According to the article, all of the following are likely to be effects of the Jasmine Revolution except:
   a) the Jasmine Revolution sends a signal to authoritarian leaders that the use of force is not enough to maintain power
   b) it shows that secular movements can also bring down governments in the region
   c) it shows that authoritarian regimes should not count on the support of western democracies to remain in power
   d) popular support is necessary to maintain power in the region
   e) the events in Tunisia will not spread unrest and revolt to neighboring countries

7 The author of the article is optimistic about the outcome of the Jasmine Revolution in the region. (C) (E)

8 The purpose of the article is to:
   a) inform readers about events in north Africa and their possible consequences for the region in the coming months
   b) convince the west to stop supporting authoritarian leaders in the region like Egypt's Mohamed Hosni Mubarak
   c) criticize the west for the errors they have made in the past in the region
   d) warn Arab nations in the region that revolution is inevitable
   e) encourage people to use violence against authoritarian governments

14

Malária e boa governança

A malária é uma doença infecciosa crônica causada por protozoários transmitidos pela picada do mosquito do gênero Anopheles. Estima-se que a doença mata 3 milhões de pessoas por ano. Em janeiro de 2011, a Organização das Nações Unidas divulgou que grande parte do dinheiro internacional arrecadado para a compra de remédios para combater a malária e outras doenças não chegara às vítimas. Ao investigar países como Haiti, Zâmbia e Mali, a ONU anunciou que os desvios já ultrapassam US$ 50 milhões no Fundo Global. O Fundo foi uma iniciativa criada com o apoio do governo brasileiro para garantir recursos para compra de remédios para o tratamento de Aids, tuberculose e malária. No artigo reproduzido a seguir, argumenta-se que os altos índices da doença em alguns países estão relacionados com a corrupção estatal.

The malaria case study: the antidote is good governance born from a strong media

1   Malaria is a case study in why good governance not just good science is the solution to so much human suffering. This year, the **mosquito borne disease** will kill over one million people. More than 80% of
5   these will be children. Great Britain used to have malaria. In North America, malaria was epidemic and there are still a handful of infections each year. In Africa malaria kills over 100 people per hour. In Russia, amidst the corruption of the 1990s, **malaria
10   re-established itself**. What is the difference between these cases?
       Why does Malaria kill so many people in one place but barely **take hold** in another? Why has malaria been allowed to **gain a foothold** in places like Russia
15   where it was previously eradicated? We know how to prevent malaria epidemics. The science is universal. The difference is good governance.

case study: estudo de caso
good governance: boa governança, bom governo
mosquito borne disease: doença transmitida por mosquitos

malaria re-established itself: a malária reestabeleceu-se

take hold: se estabelece
gain a foothold: se estabelecer

Put another way, unresponsive or corrupt government, through malaria alone, causes a children's **"9/11"** every day.

It is only when the people know the true plans and behaviour of their governments that they can meaningfully choose to support or reject them. Historically, the most resilient forms of open government are those where publication and revelation are protected. Where that protection does not exist, it is our mission to provide it through an **energetic and watchful media**.

In Kenya, malaria was estimated to cause 20% of all deaths in children under five. Before the December 2007 national elections, WikiLeaks exposed $3 billion of Kenyan corruption, which **swung the vote** by 10%. This led to changes in the constitution and the establishment of a more open government. It is too soon to know if it will contribute to a change in the human cost of malaria in Kenya but in the long term we believe it may. It is one of many **reforms catalyzed by** WikiLeaks' **unvarnished reporting**.

http://www.wikileaksdocument.com

put another way: (marcador de discurso para resumir ou concluir) em outras palavras, em resumo
"9/11": uma catástrofe (alusão aos atentados terroristas de 11 de setembro de 2001)

energetic and watchful media: uma mídia vigorosa e vigilante

swung the vote: mudou, influenciou a votação

reforms catalyzed by: reformas instigadas por
unvarnished reporting: reportagem bruta, honesta, transparente

---

A malária ou paludismo é uma doença infecciosa transmitida por mosquitos. A doença mata cerca de 3 milhões de pessoas por ano de acordo com a Organização Mundial de Saúde (OMS). Apesar de a maioria das infecções ser atualmente na África subsaariana, a doença não é exclusivamente tropical. O maior surto de malária em tempos modernos foi na Sibéria (Rússia) em 1920 e 1930, quando 13 milhões de pessoas foram infectadas.

Questions

1 According to the article, which of the following statements is true?
   a) A few cases of malaria appear in Great Britain ever year.
   b) In the 1990's, Russia was able to effectively reduce the number of malaria cases in the country.

c) Malaria is an exclusively tropical disease which explains why Africa has so many cases.
   d) Great Britain had malaria in the past but no longer does.
   e) There is no consensus on how to eradicate malaria.

2 **The expression "put another way" (line 19) can be correctly substituted by:**
   a) in other words
   b) to put it lightly
   c) however
   d) moreover
   e) this is not to say that

3 **The word "them" in the sentence "It is only when the people know the true plans and behaviour of their governments that they can meaningfully choose to support or reject *them*" refers to:**
   a) support
   b) the true plans and behaviour
   c) the people
   d) the choices

4 **The use of the modal verb "may" in the sentence "It is too soon to know if it will contribute to a change in the human cost of malaria in Kenya but in the long term we believe it *may*." expresses:**
   a) probability
   b) certainty
   c) permission
   d) obligation
   e) possibility

5 **The main purpose of the article is to:**
   a) demonstrate how a watchful media can lead to more responsible government.
   b) discuss the history of malaria.
   c) motivate readers to help in the fight against malaria in Africa.
   d) criticize governments in Africa.
   e) inform readers of the principle ways of combating the disease around the globe.

15

Julian Assange e seus críticos liberais

O site da organização WikiLeaks e seu controverso fundador, Julian Assange, foram alvos de fortes críticas na imprensa americana ao longo de 2010 em decorrência da divulgação de segredos do governo norte-americano. No artigo que segue, o jornalista Aaron Ross aponta algumas incoerências nas percepções sobre as ações da WikiLeaks.

Assange and his liberal critics

The U.S. government's **slow but steady march toward** prosecuting WikiLeaks founder Julian Assange has **picked up momentum** in recent weeks. The **Justice Department** has **subpoenaed** the Twitter account information of WikiLeaks and several of its supporters as part of its **"ongoing criminal investigation."** Facebook and Google are **rumored to** have received similar **court orders**. An **indictment** under the **Espionage Act** appears most likely, although **conspiracy charges** are **reportedly** being considered as well.

One charge the Australian Assange **won't be facing** is treason. Not that some haven't **entertained the idea**. In December, Joe Lieberman was asked on Fox News **what he made of** the Justice Department's failure to prosecute Assange as a traitor. "I'm not sure why that hasn't happened yet," Lieberman replied. His apparent belief that the United States could **slap a treason charge** on a foreign national elicited predictable **howls of derision** from liberals.

liberal: para os norte-americanos, "liberal" refere-se geralmente a pessoas de esquerda que acreditam que intervenções estatais são necessárias para o bem-estar dos indivíduos. No resto do mundo (inclusive no Brasil), "liberal" refere-se aos defensores da economia de mercado, da livre-iniciativa e do Estado mínimo.
slow but steady march toward: caminha paulatinamente na direção de
picked up momentum: ganhou impulso
Justice Department: Promotoria do Estado
subpoenaed: intimou, requisitou
ongoing criminal investigation: investigação em andamento
rumored to: supostamente
court orders: requerimentos legais
indictment: indiciação, acusação formal
Espionage Act: lei de segurança nacional norte-americana de 1917
conspiracy charges: acusações de

Even the conservative *New York Sun* **took a dig** the next day at the Connecticut senator's **cluelessness**. "**The Founders** just didn't trust the Congress [to define treason], and to listen to Senator Lieberman, one can understand why."

If a few conservatives **stood up** to defend Assange against accusations of treason, many more liberals have **blasted** him for its journalistic equivalent. Peter Beinart, former editor of *The New Republic*, condemned Assange soon after the release of the first **leaked State Department cables** for "publishing documents that sabotage American **foreign policy** without adding much, if anything, to the public debate." Jamie Rubin, a **former assistant secretary of state** during the Clinton administration, called WikiLeaks' actions "a **cyber attack** on the United States in general" for **undermining** American diplomats' relationships with global leaders.

In light of these criticisms, it is worth reiterating one basic fact: Julian Assange is Australian. How is it then that he's responsible for protecting American foreign policy interests? Suppose an American journalist published, say, Chinese diplomatic cables. Would Assange's critics find that act equally reprehensible? Of course not.

So why the **double standard**? It's quite simple, really. Assange's detractors, even those deeply critical of American policies themselves, consider U.S. foreign policy **writ large** presumptively good. **Their world exists in sharp contrasts of black and white**. Anything that undermines American foreign policy is, **therefore**, objectively bad. Call it the "you're either with us or you're against us" syndrome, version 2.0.

Take Rubin's **convoluted argument** to CNN's John Roberts on why WikiLeaks' actions are so irresponsible. "If the U.S. needs the help [...] of the leader of Yemen to attack a terrorist group planning an attack on the United States, and that leader refuses to publicly support us because of its own problems, we as Americans trying to defend our national security interests need to be able to have a

---

conjuração, conspiração contra o Estado
reportedly: supostamente
won't be facing: não vai enfrentar
entertained the idea: contemplaram a hipótese, ideia
what he made of: o que ele achou, como ele entendeu
slap a treason charge: fazer uma acusação de traição
howls of derision: gritos de escárnio, ridicularização
took a dig: criticou, provocou (informal)
cluelessness: falta de conhecimento, ignorância
The Founders: (The Founding Fathers) os "pais fundadores" dos Estados Unidos e autores da Constituição
stood up: se manifestassem
blasted: atacado
leaked State Department cables: telegramas do Departamento de Estado divulgados clandestinamente
foreign policy: política externa
former assistant secretary of state: ex-assistente secretário de Estado
cyber attack: um ataque por meio da Internet
undermining: solapando, comprometendo
in light of: à luz dos, em relação aos
double standard: dois pesos e duas medidas, ou seja, a não aplicação das mesmas regras a pessoas
writ large: em geral, em grande escala
their world exists in sharp contrasts of black and white: o mundo deles existe como um contraste nítido de preto e branco, ou seja, numa visão maniqueísta
therefore: (marcador de discurso que indica uma conclusão) portanto
convoluted argument: argumento ofuscante, sofístico

private conversation with him [...] about how to go about defending the country [...] and if that leader knows that that statement or actions that he takes privately are **going to be made public**, he may not do them, and **terrorist cells** may not be destroyed, and Americans may die because of the irresponsibility of these people."

Never mind that a number of experts have openly questioned the wisdom, not to mention the morality, of U.S. support for Yemen's corrupt and authoritarian government, which according to **Human Rights Watch** has engaged in **war crimes** in its conflicts with domestic adversaries and elements of which have been linked to al Qaeda. According to Rubin's logic, journalists must defer to the government's policy judgments and **keep their mouths shut** — even if they're Australian.

CNN's generally liberal legal analyst Jeffrey Toobin **argued as much** during an appearance on Parker/Spitzer, where he seemed to suggest that only the government is justified in disclosing classified national security information. Said Toobin, "If you intend to simply **blow out** 250,000 documents that are putting individuals at risk, the United States government employees at risk, people who cooperate with the United States government at risk — that is **not up to Julian Assange**. That is up to the United States government". (It should be noted there is positively *zero* evidence that anyone has died or been physically harmed as a result of the some 2,000 cables published so far, nor as a result of the previously leaked **field reports** from Afghanistan and Iraq.)

There are plenty of valid criticisms of Assange. He **endangered innocent lives** with the leaked field reports from Afghanistan, which failed to protect the identities of informants and other vulnerable individuals. His publication of a **college sorority**'s "secret ritual" and the **private rites** of groups including Masons and Mormons for no discernible journalistic purpose, as noted by the Federation of American Scientists' Steven Aftergood, comes across

going to be made public: serão divulgadas publicamente
terrorist cells: grupos terroristas, células terroristas

never mind that: não importa que

Human Rights Watch: ONG internacional que denuncia abusos de direitos humanos
war crimes: crimes de guerra

keep their mouths shut: calar-se, manter-se em silêncio (informal)

argued as much: repetiu o mesmo argumento

blow out: divulgar indiscriminadamente de uma vez

not up to Julian Assange: não cabe a Julian Assange

field reports: relatórios dos agentes no local

endangered innocent lives: ameaçou as vidas de pessoas inocentes

college sorority: organização social de mulheres em universidades
private rites: cerimônias secretas
churlish: bronco, tosco

as **churlish**, his belief in the virtue of near-total transparency naïve.

His refusal to **kowtow** to the expectations of American **pundits punch drunk** on some **amped-up version** of American exceptionalism, however, is not one of them. There are certain universal standards to which all journalists should be **held to account** — **accuracy in reporting**, respect for sources' confidentiality wishes, care to protect innocent life. If fidelity to American foreign policy has suddenly become another, one can hardly blame Julian Assange **if he didn't get the memo.**

AARON ROSS
http://www.worldpress.org

---

kowtow: submeter-se
pundits: especialistas
punch drunk: tonto, fora de si
amped-up version: versão exagerada
American exceptionalism: refere-se à ideia da superioridade da cultura e das instituições norte-americanas como historicamente únicas
however: (marcador de discurso para contrastar) entretanto
held to account: cobrados, julgados de acordo com certas regras
accuracy in reporting: reproduzir os fatos com fidelidade
if he didn't get the memo: se ele não foi informado sobre o assunto

---

A palavra sabotagem vem do francês *sabotage*, a partir da palavra *saboter*, que significa "estragar ou fazer de forma malfeita". Vem originalmente de *sabot*, "tamanco". O sentido moderno de "deliberada e maliciosa destruição de propriedade" originou-se durante os conflitos proletários no século XIX. Entretanto, a suposta tática de atirar sapatos velhos (ou tamancos) em máquinas industriais com o objetivo de quebrá-las não é sustentada historicamente. Provavelmente, a palavra foi usada num sentido genérico de "estragar".

Questions

1. From the first paragraph, it is clear that the United States government is:
   a) using its resources to build a legal case against Julian Assange
   b) looking to help Julian Assange
   c) keeping track of Wikileaks
   d) approaching the situation carefully
   e) being willingly helped by private organizations

2. The word "undermining" (line 37) in "undermining American diplomats' relationships" could be correctly replaced by:
   a) promoting
   b) fomenting
   c) extracting

d) compromising
  e) facilitating

3 **In the text, the author argues that it is not possible for Julian Assange to be charged with treason because:**
  a) he is not an American citizen
  b) he lives outside the United States
  c) he enjoys diplomatic immunity
  d) he is a special guy
  e) he has done nothing wrong

4 **According to the article, Assange has received criticism from many American liberals largely because:**
  a) he has not consulted the US State Department to get authorization to release the cables
  b) he has acted against what are perceived to be noble US foreign policy interests
  c) he has directly contributed to the death of Americans in Iraq and Afghanistan by releasing the identities of US officials there
  d) American liberals don't value free speech
  e) Assange is Australian and is committing treason

5 **In the sentence below, the word "its" refers to:**

*Never mind that a number of experts have openly questioned the wisdom, not to mention the morality, of U.S. support for Yemen's corrupt and authoritarian government, which according to Human Rights Watch has engaged in war crimes in **its** conflicts with domestic adversaries and elements of which have been linked to al Qaeda.*

  a) the abbreviation of "it is"
  b) a number of experts
  c) Yemen
  d) Human Rights Watch
  e) al Qaeda

6 **According to the text, the release of the diplomatic cables by Wikileaks has led directly to the death of some US government employees.** (C) (E)

7 **The main purpose of the article is to:**
  a) criticize Assange for acting against the interests of American foreign policy
  b) warn readers of the dangers of revealing sensitive information in the media

c) inform readers of the contents of the leaked cables
d) argue for the apprehension and charging of Assange for treason
e) defend Assange against unfair criticism from American liberals

Glossário dos termos mais importantes nos artigos

A seguir, encontram-se as colocações, expressões e termos mais importantes dos artigos, em ordem alfabética. O leitor deve conhecer esse vocabulário, que aparece frequentemente em artigos sobre atualidades e textos de concursos.

9/11: a data 11 de setembro de 2001, quando aconteceram os ataques terroristas nos EUA
absence of rule of law: ausência de um Estado de Direito, literalmente, sem lei
accuracy in reporting: reproduzir os fatos com fidelidade
action-oriented dialogue: um diálogo com objetivos práticos
ad hoc: sem planejamento; no contexto jurídico, a palavra é usada no sentido de "para esta finalidade"
address: abordar, lidar com
all-out: sem restrições, no sentido de fazer algo "sem reservas"
American exceptionalism: refere-se à ideia da superioridade da cultura e das instituições norte-americanas
annual growth rates: taxas de crescimento anuais
anti-western: contra o Ocidente, contra os valores do Ocidente
around the globe: ao redor do mundo, internacionalmente
ask (the) hard questions: desafiar, literalmente, fazer perguntas difíceis ou desafiadoras
at the expense of their own people: às custas de seu próprio povo
authority structures: instituições, estruturas de autoridades estatais
average income: renda média
backed by oil: garantia de conversibilidade por petróleo
backing of U.S. dollars by gold: garantia de conversibilidade por ouro
balance of power: balanço de poder
ballooning government deficits: dívidas públicas em rápida expansão

ban access: restringir, proibir o acesso
bankruptcy: falência
bear fruit: dar resultados
become privy: ficar sabendo, ter acesso a
beggar thy neighbor: estratégia de empobrecer o seu vizinho num jogo de soma zero
beginning of the end: o começo do fim
behind closed doors: em segredo
bipartisan presidential panel: um painel presidencial com membros dos dois maiores partidos
blast: atacar verbalmente, criticar severamente
boiling angry: furioso
boost currencies: valorizar moedas
boost the economy: elevar o nível da produção
breed discontent: fomentar a infelicidade
Bretton Woods: tratado internacional que estabeleceu a arquitetura econômica e financeira após a Segunda Guerra Mundial definindo um sistema de regras, instituições e procedimentos para regular a política econômica internacional
bring the troops home: tirar as tropas do campo, trazê-las de volta ao país
bring to power: levar ao poder
by-product: consequência
cables: telegramas, comunicações
campaign slogan: breve e incisiva frase publicitária de campanha
capital controls: controle de capitais
capital flight: fuga de capitais
carbon and methane emissions: emissões de dióxido de carbono e de gás metano
carry trade: prática de pegar dinheiro emprestado em um país com juros baixos e aplicá-lo em um país com juros altos
causal link: ligação causal
cease to exist: desaparecer, deixar de existir
change of mind: mudança de ideia, adotar novo conceito
citizenry: conjunto de cidadãos, público
citizenship: cidadania
civil society: sociedade civil
clash of civilisations: expressão usada pela primeira vez por Bernard Lewis em 1990 em artigo sobre o sentimento de ódio de muitos no mundo islâmico pelas ações norte-americanas. O termo entrou em voga após o ensaio de Samuel Huntington, intitulado "O choque das civilizações".
clear and present: óbvio e iminente, claro e real
clear message: mensagem clara
clear warning message: um aviso claro
clear-cut answers: respostas claras e concisas
clearly articulated vision: visão claramente articulada

collapse into civil war: desintegrar em guerra civil
collective goal: objetivo coletivo
come of age: amadurecer
conditional cash-transfer program: programa assistencialista condicionado
conspiracy charges: acusações de conjuração, conspiração contra o Estado
containment: a contenção foi uma política dos Estados Unidos durante a Guerra Fria que usava estratégias militares, econômicas e diplomáticas contra a propagação do comunismo no âmbito internacional
core argument: argumento central
core inflation: uma das estatísticas usadas para medir o aumento do nível de preços no "cerne" (core) da economia, que tipicamente não leva em consideração alimentos ou energia
corridors of power: bastidores do poder
cost-effective: algo que pode ser justificado economicamente por ter retornos previstos maiores que os investimentos
cost-of-living increase: reajuste de acordo com o aumento do nível de preços
court orders: requerimentos legais
create at will: criar arbitrariamente
criminal charges: acusações criminais
currency wars: "guerra de moedas", uma desvalorização competitiva das moedas nacionais
cushion the blow: amenizar o problema
cyber attack: ataque por meio da Internet
day-to-day goods: bens de consumo básicos, como alimentos e combustível
deadlocked: sem acordo, travado politicamente
decouple: desvincular
deep roots: raízes profundas
deeply regret: lamentar profundamente
deep-rooted: enraizado
default on a payment: dar calote numa dívida; não pagar os juros para manter a dívida
democratisation "from below": processo democrático que vem das camadas sociais mais populares. Em inglês, usa-se frequentemente a expressão "grass roots" para designar tais movimentos.
depreciated dollars: dólares depreciados
destruction of habitat: destruição de ecossistema(s)
deteriorating debt repayment capability: uma capacidade deteriorada de ressarcir os credores
deteriorating living conditions: qualidade de vida em deterioração
devalue a currency: desvalorizar intencionalmente a moeda
development agenda: agenda política sobre o desenvolvimento
development assistance: ajuda para o desenvolvimento

dire economic situations: situações econômicas precárias ou difíceis
diversified agricultural economy: diversificada economia baseada na agricultura
dollar holdings: reservas em dólar
domestic norms: leis nacionais
domestic regime: governo, regime nacional
domestic slavery: escravidão no país
doomed to poverty: condenados a uma vida de pobreza
double standard: dois pesos e duas medidas, ou seja, a não aplicação das mesmas regras a pessoas diferentes
draft resolution: proposta de resolução (da Organização das Nações Unidas)
drain economic resources: acabar com recursos econômicos
drastic spending cuts: grandes cortes no orçamento
drive down the value of the dollar: reduzir (propositalmente) o valor do dólar
drug czar: oficial do governo norte-americano responsável pela elaboração e gerenciamento das políticas de repressão contra às drogas ilícitas
drug warriors: pessoas que sustentam a política de repressão contra drogas ilícitas
economic backwardness: atraso econômico
economic contraction: contração da economia
economic goods: bens de consumo
economic performance: desempenho da economia
economic policies: políticas econômicas
economic snake oil remedy: uma falsa cura econômica
economic stagnation: estagnação econômica
economically speaking: em relação à economia
electoral politics: processo político democrático
elite pacts: arranjos políticos entre as elites
empower citizens: capacitar os cidadãos, empoderar
endanger innocent lives: ameaçar as vidas de pessoas inocentes
energetic and watchful media: uma mídia vigorosa e vigilante
enjoy freedom of expression: gozar de liberdade de expressão
entertain an idea: contemplar uma hipótese ou ideia
entrepreneurs: empreendedores
environmental activist: ambientalista
environmental sustainability: preservação do meio ambiente
erode the standard of living: prejudicar a qualidade de vida
Espionage Act: lei de segurança nacional norte-americana de 1917
established order: a estrutura de poder vigente
ever-depreciating dollars: dólares cada vez mais depreciados
exchange rates: taxas de câmbio
expansion of the money supply: aumento da quantidade de dinheiro pelo governo
expatriate: expatriado, emigrante
expropriate assets: expropriar ou confiscar bens

extract resources: extrair recursos
extreme inequality: desigualdade extrema
failing states: Estados fracassados
fall under the general rubric: encaixar na categoria geral
false messiahs: profetas falsos
Fed Chairman: diretor do banco central norte-americano
federal spending cuts: cortes nos gastos federais
fiat currency: moeda nacional sem lastro ou conversibilidade em ouro, outro metal ou commodity
fiat monetary system: sistema monetário no qual a moeda nacional não tem lastro ou conversibilidade em ouro, outro metal ou commodity
field reports: relatórios dos agentes no local
fill public coffers: encher os cofres públicos
final round: segundo turno nas eleições
finance: a área financeira
financial meltdown: colapso do sistema financeiro
financial rescue package: pacote de ajuda ao sistema financeiro
financial sector: setor financeiro
financier: homem das altas finanças
first round: primeiro turno
fiscal discipline: disciplina fiscal
fiscal profligacy: desperdício do dinheiro público
fizzle: fracassar
flood financial markets: inundar mercados financeiros
focus on: concentrar-se em
follow suit: seguir o exemplo
foreign aid: ajuda humanitária
foreign policy: política exterior, política externa
former colony: ex-colônia
free and unrestrained press: imprensa livre e sem restrições
free electoral process: processo eleitoral livre e democrático
freedom of information laws: leis que garantem o acesso às informações do governo
free-market ideologues: proponentes das ideias do "mercado livre" (a palavra "ideologue" tem um sentido pejorativo)
from that standpoint: a partir desse ponto de vista
fuel social change: promover mudança social
fundamentalist Muslims: muçulmanos fundamentalistas
Funny-Money: dinheiro falso (expressão informal)
G20 economic summit: reunião econômica dos países do grupo G20
gain a foothold: se estabelecer
gain momentum: ganhar impulso
gain the upper hand: ganhar uma posição de vantagem

gamble: apostar
gather in public: reunir-se em público
GDP: sigla de "gross domestic product", produto interno bruto (PIB)
generating capacity: capacidade de geração de energia
get on the right track economically: tomar o rumo econômico correto
go beyond: ir além
good bargain: um bom negócio
good governance: boa governança, bom governo
good name: boa reputação
goods: bens, produtos
governance issues: questões de governança
grand strategy: estratégia abrangente
grant asylum: conceder asilo político
grassroots: relativo aos cidadãos comuns
Great Depression: a grande depressão econômica que começou com a quebra da Bolsa de Nova Iorque em 1929
Greater Middle East: neologismo da administração Bush para se referir a um grupo de países islâmicos além do Oriente Médio, e que inclui a Turquia, Irã, Afeganistão e Paquistão
great-power nations: as grandes potências, nações dominantes no cenário internacional
Green Party: Partido Verde
gross dishonesty: grande desonestidade
gross oversimplification: uma simplificação exagerada
growth rates: taxas de crescimento
growth: crescimento, crescimento econômico
guide policy: balizar as políticas públicas
hand over: entregar
have nothing to do: não têm nada a ver
heavy hand: com o uso de força
heavy state control: controle estatal rígido e pesado
held to account: cobrado, julgado de acordo com certas regras
high cost of living: alto custo de vida
high finance: altas finanças
high unemployment: alta taxa de desemprego
highlight: enfatizar, salientar
highly volatile capital flows: fluxo de capitais altamente volátil
highly correlated: com uma alta correlação, interligados
hoard information: segurar informações
hope springs eternal: nunca se perde a esperança
hot money: capitais especulativos
howls of derision: gritos de escárnio, ridicularização

human development indicators: indicadores de desenvolvimento social
Human Rights Watch: ONG internacional que denuncia abusos de direitos humanos
human rights: direitos humanos
humanise politics: humanizar a política
IMF: Fundo Monetário Internacional (FMI)
implement policies: implementar políticas públicas
improve living standards: melhorar a qualidade de vida
in light of: à luz dos, em relação aos
in the grand scheme: em geral, numa perspectiva ampla
increasingly important: cada vez mais importante
indictment: indiciação, acusação formal
Industrial Revolution: Revolução Industrial
inequality in income distribution: desigualdade na distribuição de renda
infeasible: inviável
inflation fears: o medo da inflação
inflation tax: um "imposto inflacionário"
inflationary policies: políticas inflacionárias
institutional constraints: limitações institucionais
intellectual property rights: direito de propriedade intelectual
intellectually wrongheaded: intelectualmente equivocado
international coverage: cobertura na mídia internacional
international environment: cenário internacional
international monetary system: o sistema monetário internacional
interoceanic trade: comércio marítimo interoceânico, entre vários continentes
investment barriers: barreiras aos investimentos (especificamente aos capitais especulativos)
investors seek higher returns: investidores procuram retornos mais elevados
iron-clad arrangement: um acordo sólido, que não poderia ser quebrado
irresponsible sovereigns: governos irresponsáveis
is more likely: é mais provável
Jasmine Revolution: revolta popular na Tunísia em janeiro de 2011 que levou à expulsão do ditador daquele país
Justice Department: Promotoria do Estado norte-americano
keep their mouths shut: calar-se, manter-se em silêncio (informal)
kleptocracy: governo corrupto, cleptocracia; refere-se a um regime político-social em que predominam as práticas corruptas
kowtow: submeter-se
labor market institutions: instituições relacionadas ao mercado de trabalho, trabalhistas
labor union leader: líder de sindicato trabalhista
labor unions: sindicatos
lack of opportunity: falta de oportunidades

landmark ruling: decisão jurídica importante
last hope: a última esperança
lead to the collapse: levar ao colapso, implosão, dissolução
leading business: indústria mais importante
leading up to: que precedeu
leak: divulgar clandestinamente
levels of prosperity: níveis de riqueza
life-expectancy rates: taxas de expectativa de vida
lift America out of recession: estimular a economia americana a sair da recessão
live on less than $1 a day: sobrevivem com menos de um dólar por dia
live up to the rhetoric: corresponder à altura do discurso oficial
living standards: padrões de vida
low expectation: baixa expectativa
low returns on US bonds: baixos retornos nos títulos do governo norte-americano
low wages: salários baixos
major challenges: grandes desafios
major fumbles: grandes erros
make no mistake: não se iluda
make something public: divulgar publicamente
make a lot of sense: fazer sentido
male suffrage: sufrágio (direito de voto) para todos os homens
malevolent dictators: ditadores maldosos, malevolentes
manipulate currency: manipular moeda
massive popular support: apoio popular maciço
masters of their destiny: dono de seu próprio destino
matter of grave concern: um assunto seriíssimo
mean business: estar sério
meet something with ridicule: ridicularizar
metalworker: torneiro mecânico
middle and upperclass fear: o medo da classe média e da elite dominante (classe dominante)
Middle Easterner: indivíduo do Oriente Médio
midterm elections: eleições legislativas dois anos após o começo do mandato presidencial norte-americano
mid-twentieth century: meados do século vinte
military budget: orçamento militar
military coup: golpe militar
military overstretch: excessivamente engajado com as forças armadas
minimal institutional architecture: um arcabouço institucional mínimo
mint coins: cunhar moedas (de metal)
miserable pittance: quantia pequena, mixaria
mission accomplished: missão cumprida

missteps: erros
mockery: gozação ou zombaria
model of growth: modelo de crescimento econômico
mold the international environment: moldar o ambiente internacional
monetary base: a base monetária, ou seja, a quantidade total de dinheiro impresso pelo governo
monetary policy: política monetária
monopoly money: dinheiro de brincadeira, como usado no jogo Banco Imobiliário
moral outrage: revolta (sentir-se revoltado moralmente)
mortgage deductions: isenção de imposto sobre hipotecas
mosquito borne disease: doença transmitida por mosquitos
move towards: caminhando em direção a algo
much of the rest of the world: grande parte do resto do mundo
multiparty system: sistema pluripartidário
multiple layers of conflict: conflitos complexos que não podem ser reduzidos a apenas uma causa
mutually beneficial agreements: acordos mutuamente benéficos
mutually beneficial bargains: barganhas ou arranjos mutuamente benéficos
nation-state: Estado-nação, Estado
native peoples: povos indígenas
necessary condition for: uma condição necessária para
negotiated diplomatic solution: solução diplomática negociada
negotiated solution: solução negociada
New World: o Novo Mundo, as Américas
nuclear program: programa nuclear
odd political arrangements: alianças políticas oportunistas
oil fields: campos petrolíferos
Oil for Food Program: programa da Organização das Nações Unidas que permitiria que o Iraque vendesse petróleo no mercado mundial em troca de comida, remédios e outros suprimentos de valor humanitário
on the verge of civil war: à beira de uma guerra civil
once mighty: que era uma vez forte
ongoing criminal investigation: uma investigação em andamento
ongoing uncertainty: prevalecem incertezas
OPEC: abreviação de "Organization of the Petroleum Exporting Countries", Organização dos Países Exportadores de Petróleo (OPEP)
open markets: abrir mercados
open windows on the past: explorar a história, debruçar-se sobre o passado, revelar o passado
ordinary people: pessoas comuns
orienting principle: princípios que servem de guia
oust a regime from power: derrubar um regime do poder

outcries: gritos
outstanding debt: dívidas
overthrow a dictator: derrubar um ditador
panicky politicians: políticos apavorados
paradigm: paradigma, modelo
parchment institutions: instituições ou regras que só existem no papel, letra morta
parliamentary democracy: democracia parlamentarista
participatory democratic politics: políticas democráticas participativas
Party of the Brazilian Social Democracy: *Partido da Social Democracia Brasileira* (PSDB)
patent law: lei de patentes
pave the way to: facilitar, abrir caminho para
peaceful purposes: propósitos pacíficos
people's empowerment: empoderamento do povo, democratização
per capita income: renda per capita (por pessoa)
pet projects: projetos favoritos
pick up momentum: ganhar impulso
plant: usina (hidrelétrica, nuclear etc.)
play a bigger role: desempenhar um papel maior
play a fundamental role: desempenhar um papel fundamental
play a key role/ play a vital role: desempenhar um papel fundamental
play into the hands of: favorecer um ponto de vista
pledge: prometer
plunder: roubar
policy initiatives: iniciativas de programas sociais
policy makers: formuladores de políticas públicas
political developments: mudanças políticas
political liberalisation: liberalização política
political malaise: mal-estar político
political momentum: tendência política
political obstacles: obstáculos políticos
political sacred cows: programas políticos considerados politicamente intocáveis
political support: apoio político
politically incorrect: politicamente incorreto
poor investment ratings: baixa classificação nos índices de investimentos internacionais
poorly performing economies: economias com baixo desempenho
potential candidate: uma possível opção
poverty levels: níveis de pobreza
price controls: controle governamental de preços
principal crafter: autor principal
private investment: investimentos privados
private property rights: direitos de propriedade

private rites: cerimônias secretas
privileged position: posição privilegiada
profit-taking: realização de lucros pela venda de algo
promising candidate: um candidato promissor
promote de facto checks and balances on rulers: estabelecer contrapesos verdadeiros aos governantes
property rights: direitos de propriedade
pro-western: a favor do Ocidente
public goods: bens públicos
public health problem: questão de saúde pública
public scrutiny: escrutínio público, examinação pública
public services: serviços públicos
public works program: investimentos em infraestrutura (obras públicas)
publicly downgrade America's credit rating: rebaixar publicamente a avaliação em relação à capacidade do governo americano em cobrir as suas dívidas
punch drunk: tonto, fora de si
pundits: especialistas (muitas vezes usado de forma pejorativa)
punitive action: ação punitiva
quantitative easing (QE): refere-se a uma política monetária que visa aumentar a quantidade de dinheiro
rapid economic growth: crescimento econômico acelerado
real inflation/ true inflation: inflação verdadeira
receive the political recognition it deserves: receber o reconhecimento político que merece
recent social improvements: melhorias sociais recentes
reduce the national deficit: reduzir a dívida pública federal
reduction of greenhouse gases: redução de gases do efeito estufa
regime change: expressão usada nos Estados Unidos desde 1925 para se referir à mudança de governos e instituições em outros países. Tornou-se amplamente usada nos governos Clinton e Bush para definir a política norte-americana em relação ao Estado iraquiano.
regulate international regimes: controlar governos no âmbito internacional
regulatory environment: ambiente regulatório (estrutura jurídica)
repay creditors: ressarcir os credores
reserve currency: moeda(s) usada(s) pelos Estados para suas reservas internacionais
responsible sovereignty: soberania responsável
review process: estudos de viabilidade e de impacto social e ambiental
rife with corruption: com alto índice de corrupção
rigid social stratification: estratificação social rígida
ripple effect: um efeito que se espalha
rise of fundamentalism: a ascendência do fundamentalismo
risk life and limb: arriscar a vida

role of property rights: papel desempenhado pelo direito de propriedade
Roosevelt: Franklin Delano Roosevelt, presidente norte-americano entre 1933 e 1945
rudderless: sem direção, sem leme
ruling party: o partido no poder
rumored to: supostamente
run contrary to: contraria
run down the US dollar: rebaixar o valor do dólar norte-americano
run the country into the ground: quebrar o país, levando-o à falência
save their skins: salvarem-se
savers: as pessoas que pouparam dinheiro ao longo da vida
scare tactic: ameaças fictícias
scorn: rejeitar
secure votes: assegurar votos
Security Council: Conselho de Segurança das Nações Unidas
send the wrong signal: confundir, enganar, mandar o sinal errado
set an example: dar um exemplo
settler mortality data: dados (estatísticas) sobre a mortalidade dos colonizadores
share the same vision: compartilhar a mesma visão
shellacked by voters: surrado nas urnas
shift the true costs to the tax-payers: repassar os custos verdadeiros aos contribuintes
Shock-and-Awe: ações bélicas de grande força destrutiva visando causar efeitos psicológicos
short- or medium-term: de curto ou médio prazo
short-term investment: investimentos de curto prazo
silver bullet: solução fácil
siphon off (money): desviar dinheiro
sit-ins: protestos pacíficos com a ocupação de um local
slap in the face: tapa na cara, injúria, insulto
slave trade: comércio de escravos
slum movements: movimentos populares
so-called: suposto, chamado (usado de forma irônica)
social security checks: pagamento de aposentadorias
social security: programa de apoio social
sound, commodity-backed money: moeda forte com garantia de conversibilidade em alguma commodity (matérias-primas) como ouro
spark riots: desencadear protestos violentos
spat: briga, conflito
spin: informações enganosas e manipuladas
stage a war: iniciar uma guerra
state intelligence agencies: órgãos de inteligência estatais
stem from: originar-se de

stimulate the economy: estimular a economia
stinging rebuke: forte repreensão, exprobração
stoke worldwide inflation: fomentar a inflação monetária global
strong institutions: instituições sólidas, confiáveis
strongmen: líderes autoritários
subpoena: intimação judicial
sub-saharan Africa: África subsaariana
subsidized loans: empréstimos subsidiados
superpowers: nações hegemônicas
supreme goal: o objetivo principal
sweeten the deal: melhorar a proposta
swing the vote: influenciar a votação
symbols of status/ status symbols: símbolos de status
take a dig: criticar, provocar (informal)
take advantage: aproveitar
take as given: subentender
take hold: se estabelecer
tantamount to a tax: efetivamente um imposto
targeted policies: políticas com alvo específico
tax incentives: incentivos fiscais
tax: tributar, cobrar impostos
tax: imposto
tear down: derrubar
Tehran Declaration: declaração conjunta controversa do Brasil, Turquia e Irã propondo a troca de materiais nucleares
terrorist cells: grupos terroristas, células terroristas
the centerpiece: o pilar central
the elusive Holy Grail: o santo remédio elusivo (Holy Grail, o "Cálice Sagrado" usado na Última Ceia, refere-se a um objetivo quase impossível de ser realizado, mas que seria de grande benefício para a humanidade)
the Fed: forma abreviada do nome do banco central norte-americano (Federal Reserve), normalmente usado com o artigo "the"
The Founders: os "pais fundadores" dos Estados Unidos e autores da Constituição norte-americana
the House: Câmara dos Deputados
the West: o Ocidente
those on fixed incomes: aqueles que vivem de aposentadorias, pensões e outras fontes de renda fixa
throw money at something: investir dinheiro cegamente em algo
throwing aid money: gastar grandes quantidades de dinheiro em África, para fins humanitários
tie (a currency) to gold: atrelar (uma moeda) ao ouro

time and again: muitas vezes
topple a regime: derrubar um regime/ governo
trade openness: abertura ao comércio
trade: comerciar
trade: comércio
tragic consequences: consequências trágicas
transformative power of politics: força transformadora da política
Treasury Department: instituição governamental norte-americana que emite moeda e títulos
turn one's back (on something/ someone): rejeitar, virar as costas, não apoiar, abandonar
U.S. imperial tax: "imposto imperial" norte-americano
U.S. Secretary of State: secretária do Departamento de Estado (chefe da Casa Civil norte-americana)
UN: abreviação de "United Nations" (Organização das Nações Unidas)
unconstrained by checks and balances: não eram limitados por contrapesos
undermine the world's economic order: solapar a ordem (estrutura) econômica internacional
undermine: solapar
understate: subestimar
unfair colonial order: uma estrutura colonial injusta
unforeseen challenges: desafios imprevistos
unfortunate episode: um acontecimento lamentável
unique fish species: espécies de peixe únicas
United Nations' Millennium Development Goals: as Metas de Desenvolvimento do Milênio (MDM) surgem da Declaração do Milênio das Nações Unidas, adotada pelos 191 estados membros no ano de 2000
unvarnished reporting: reportagem bruta, honesta, transparente
upheaval among the poor: levante ou rebelião dos pobres
uprising: levante popular
upstream dams: represas adicionais rio acima
US debt: a dívida do governo norte-americano
US public debt: dívida pública norte-americana
US Supreme Court: supremo tribunal federal norte-americano
US (United States): Estados Unidos
vast mass of individuals: grande maioria das pessoas
verifiable assurances: meios seguros de verificar
Wall Street: centro das finanças norte-americanas, localizado na cidade de Nova Iorque
war crimes: crimes de guerra
war on drugs: "guerra contra as drogas", política norte-americana de controle às drogas via repressão policial e ações militares em outros países

war on terror: "grerra contra o terror", expressão norte-americana relacionada principalmente às ações militares daquele Estado em vários países, como no Iraque e no Afeganistão
wave of social conservatism: uma onda de conservadorismo
weak institutions: instituições fracas
well-known actors: participantes bem conhecidos
wholesale collapse: um colapso generalizado
whopping: incrível, surpreendente
wide range of issue areas: amplo espectro de assuntos
widely dispersed: amplamente distribuídas
widely used: amplamente usados
wire service: distribuidora de notícias
with all their heart: de forma veemente
Workers' Party candidate: candidato do Partido dos Trabalhadores
World Bank: Banco Mundial
world exchange rates: taxas de câmbio internacionais
world financial and currency instability: instabilidade financeira e monetária internacional
world's premier medium of exchange: moeda padrão no comércio internacional
worsening human rights conditions: condições de direitos humanos em deterioração
worthless dollars: dólares sem valor
writ large: em geral, em grande escala
wrongheaded economic response: respostas governamentais equivocadas
WWII: abreviação de "World War II", a Segunda Guerra Mundial

Glossário de marcadores de discurso

Marcadores de discurso refere-se a linguagem altamente convencionada que usamos para organizar e sinalizar o discurso. Eles são os sinais que nos dizem o que esperar pela frente. Ou seja, marcadores de discurso nos dizem o que o falante ou autor está prestes a dizer, se vai chegar a uma conclusão (logo, portanto), se está resumindo (em suma, em poucas palavras), comparando ou contrastando (por um lado... por outro lado, isso contrasta com...) ou qualquer outra importante função comunicativa. Conhecendo estes marcadores de discurso você melhorará significativamente a sua compreensão da leitura.

Abaixo compilamos um glossário com alguns dos marcadores de discurso usados com mais frequência na comunicação escrita, especialmente em textos jornalísticos como os reproduzidos neste livro.

Introduzindo novas ideias/ iniciando o discurso

first of all... ; in the first place... ; to begin with...
em primeiro lugar... ; antes de tudo... ; para começar...
in order to... ; in order that... ; so that... ; in an effort to...
com o objetivo de... ; a fim de... ; para que... ; para...
a further example (of this) is...
um outro exemplo disso seria...
another aspect of the problem is...
um outro aspecto do problema é...
another point worth considering/ analysing is...
um outro ponto que deve ser considerado/ analisado é...
as well as...; besides...; in addition (to)
além de...; adicionalmente
equally
igualmente

it is worth remembering that… ; it should not be forgotten that… ; one should remember that…
    cabe recordar que… ; cabe lembrar que… ; vale lembrar que…

which brings me/ us to my/ our next point
    o que me/ nos leva ao meu/ nosso próximo ponto

Fazendo referência / atribuindo ideias a alguém

from the standpoint of…
    do ponto de vista de…

based on the assumption that…
    pressupondo que…

from my (his/ her etc.) standpoint/ point of view…
    do meu ponto de vista…

regarding…; with regard to…; concerning…; considering…; in reference to…
    com relação a…; no que diz respeito a… ; no que tange a…

according to…; in accordance with…
    de acordo com…; conforme…

he (she/ Dr. Priscilla etc.) once said/ pointed out/ remarked /wrote that…
    ele (ela/ Dra. Priscilla etc.) disse/ apontou/ salientou/ escreveu que…

according to his (her/ their etc.) theory…
    de acordo com a teoria dele (dela/ deles etc.)…

an issue that has caused a great deal of controversy is…
    uma questão que tem sido controversa é…

common sense suggests that…
    o senso comum sugere que…

in order to analyse… it is helpful/ useful/ necessary to…
    para analisar a… seria útil/ necessário…

it is a possibility that…
    é uma possibilidade que…

one of the most complex contemporary questions is…
    uma das questões mais complexas da atualidade é…

the principle of… is widely accepted
    o princípio de… é amplamente aceito

the question of… has often been discussed
    a questão de… tem sido frequentemente discutida/ abordada

there is a widely held view/ idea that…
    há uma visão/ ideia amplamente difundida de que…

Exemplificando

the case/ the example of... (dramatically) illustrates...
  o caso/ exemplo de... comprova/ demonstra (claramente)...

an example (of this) is/ would be...
  um exemplo (disso) é/ seria...

for example; for instance
  por exemplo

for one thing... for another
  por exemplo/ de um lado... por outro lado

in the case of...
  no caso de...

it is worth considering/ mentioning the case of...
  vale considerar/ mencionar o caso de...

let us examine/ consider the case of...
  vamos examinar/ considerar o caso de...

take the case of...
  considere o caso de...

the case of... illustrates/ could be taken to illustrate...
  o caso de... mostra que/ ilustra...

the case of... provides a clear example/ graphic illustration of...
  o caso de... fornece um exemplo claro de...

this raises the question/ problem of...
  isso levanta a questão/ o problema de...

Comparando e contrastando

if one compares... with...
  quando se compara... com...

when... is compared to...
  quando... é comparado com...

when set alongside...
  quando comparado a...

compared with/ to...; in comparison with... ; as compared to...
  comparado com...

both... and...
  ambos... e...; tanto... quanto...

neither... nor...
  nem... nem...

the same as...
    igual a...
in the same way
    da mesma forma
by the same token; similarly
    da mesma forma
likewise
    também a mesma coisa
whereas
    enquanto; ao passo que
this is in (clear/ sharp) contrast to/with...
    isso contrasta (nitidamente) com...
and vice versa
    e vice versa
on the one hand... on the other hand...
    de um lado... por outro lado...
all the same
    de qualquer maneira
although
    embora
apart from
    além do...; além disso; tirando o...
at first glance it might appear that...
    inicialmente parece que...
conversely
    em contraste; por outro lado
despite; in spite of
    a despeito de
even if we accepted the idea/ argument/ proposition (that)...
    mesmo se aceitássemos a ideia/ o argumento/ a proposta (que)...
even though; still
    embora; ainda que; mesmo que
except for
    com exceção de
however
    entretanto
instead of...; rather than...
    ao invés de...
meanwhile
    enquanto nesse meio-tempo
nevertheless; nonetheless; even so; still
    mesmo assim

notwithstanding
    apesar de desconsiderando
on the contrary
    pelo contrário
the issue/ problem is not... (but) rather/ on the contrary it is...
    o problema/ a questão não é... (mas) pelo contrário é...
there is a clear distinction/ sharp contrast between...
    há uma clara distinção entre...
unlike
    diferente de
while; whereas; by contrast
    enquanto; ao passo que; já
while many people hold the view/ advocate the idea/ genuinely believe that...
    embora muitas pessoas acreditem/ apoiem a ideia de que...
with the exception of
    com a exceção de

Generalizando

as a (general) rule
    de forma geral; como regra geral
for the most part
    em geral; de forma geral
generally; in general
    geralmente; em geral
in many/ most cases...
    em muitos/ na maioria dos casos...
it is a well-known fact that...
    todo mundo sabe que...; é claro que...
it is generally/ widely believed that...
    há um consenso de que...
it is often/ usually the case that...
    frequentemente/ usualmente é o caso que...
there is a general consensus that...
    há um consenso geral de que...
whenever
    sempre que; cada vez que

Especulando/ fazendo hipóteses/ expressando possibilidade ou incerteza

conceivably
    possivelmente; há a possibilidade de que...
considering (that)...
    considerando...; levando em conta que...
given that...
    sabendo que...
imagine (that)... ; it is possible that... ; it is possible to imagine that...
    imaginando que... ; supondo que... ; contemplando que...
on condition that...
    na condição que...
possibly
    possivelmente
suppose (that)... ; supposing (that)...
    vamos supor que... ; supondo que...
taking... into consideration
    levando... em consideração
unless
    ao não ser que
in all probability
    é provável que...; provavelmente...
it is not clear why/ if/ whether/ that...
    não está claro porque/ se/ que...
it is possible/ probable that...
    é possivel/ provável que...
it may be that...
    pode ser que...
it remains to be seen whether...
    ainda vamos ver se...
perhaps
    pode ser que; possivelmente

Iniciando sequência/ enumerando

afterwards
    depois
at the same time
    ao mesmo tempo

at/ from the outset
desde o início

before that; beforehand; earlier
antes (disso)

eventually
no fim; finalmente

finally
finalmente

first and foremost
acima de tudo

first of all; in the first place
em primeiro lugar

first(ly); second(ly); third(ly)
em primeiro lugar; em segundo lugar; em terceiro lugar

in the long term/ run
no longo prazo

in the medium term
no médio prazo

in the short term/ run
no curto prazo

in the meantime
enquanto (isso)

last(ly); finally
finalmente; no final; afinal; enfim; em conclusão

meanwhile
enquanto

previously
anteriormente; antes

simultaneously
ao mesmo tempo; simultaneamente

subsequently
subsequentemente

the least important
o menos importante

the most important
o mais importante

the second/ third (etc.) most important
o segundo/ terceiro (etc.) mais importante

to begin with; to start with; in the first place
para começar; em primeiro lugar

Expressando certeza/ enfatizando

of course; for sure; definitely; certainly; without a doubt...
   com certeza; certamente; sem dúvida...
as a matter of fact...; in fact...
   de fato...
actually
   em verdade; na verdade
especially... ; mainly...
   especialmente...
in particular...
   particularmente; especificamente
certainly
   com certeza; certamente
clearly...; it can be clearly seen that...
   claramente... ; é claro que...
it has been clearly shown that...
   tem sido amplamente comprovado/ demonstrado que...
it is certain that... ; it is clear that...
   é uma certeza que... ; é claro que...
most certainly
   certamente
obviously
   obviamente
there is clear evidence that...
   há provas irrefutáveis de que...
everything points to...
   tudo indica que...
there is can be no doubt that...
   não há dúvida de que...; não tem como negar que...
undoubtedly
   sem dúvida
surely
   certamente
evidently
   evidentemente; parece que...

Resumindo/ concluindo

all things considered... ; in summary...
    levando tudo em consideração... ; resumindo...
finally; at last
    por fim; finalmente; por último
in other words...
    em outras palavras...
that is...
    ou seja...
therefore; thus; so
    portanto; então; ou seja
for this reason... ; that's why...
    por essa razão/ esse motivo... ; por isso que...
as a result of... ; due to...
    como consequência/ resultado... ; devido a/ ao...
it can be seen that...
    nota-se que...; podemos observar que...
it is obviously true that...
    é claro/ óbvio que...
all in all
    de forma geral; no final das contas
all the evidence suggests that...
    tudo indica que...
all things considered, the solution/ answer may be...
    levando tudo em consideração, a solução/ resposta pode ser...
as has been seen...
    como foi visto/ constatado...
in a nutshell...; in short...; to sum up...
    em resumo; resumindo...
in conclusion
    concluindo; em conclusão...
the main conclusion to be/ that can be drawn is that...
    a conclusão que podemos tirar é que...
as a consequence of... ; as a result of...
    como consequência de... ; como resultado de...
because
    porque
because of
    por causa de
given that...
    uma vez que... ; em decorrência de que... ; porque...

it goes without saying that...
    é óbvio que... ; está subentendido que... ; não há dúvida que...
it is for this/ that reason that...
    é por causa disso/ daquilo que...
on account of...
    devido a... ; por causa de...
owing to...
    em decorrência de...
since
    já que; desde que
this/ that is why...
    é por isso que...
the main consequence (of this) is...
    a consequência principal (disso) é...
the problem has its origins in/ stems from...
    o problema decorre de/ é causado por...
the root of the problem is...
    a origem do problema é...
this leads/ gives rise to...
    isso causa...

Respostas dos exercícios

1

1. a
2. e
3. b
4. a
5. c
6. d
7. E
8. a
9. C
10. e
11. b

2

1. c
2. a
3. d
4. e
5. a
6. b
7. b
8. d
9. c
10. a. C; b. E; c. C; d. C
11. d

3

1. b
2. a
3. a. C; b. C; c. C; d. E
4. d
5. c
6. c
7. a
8. a. C; b. C; c. E; d. E
9. a. C; b. C; c. E; d. C

4

1. d
2. a
3. a. C; b. C; c. C; d. C; e. C
4. b
5. c
6. a
7. c
8. c
9. a
10. d
11. b
12. a. C; b. E; c. C; d. C; e. C; f. E

5

1. a
2. c
3. b
4. a
5. c
6. c
7. c
8. a
9. d

6

1. b
2. e
3. a
4. a
5. c
6. d
7. a
8. d

7

1. a
2. b
3. **a.** E; **b.** C
4. C
5. **a.** C; **b.** E; **c.** C; **d.** C
6. E
7. a

8

1. E
2. d
3. b
4. c
5. E
6. C
7. C
8. d
9. C
10. C

9

1. C
2. C
3. a
4. b
5. C
6. E
7. C
8. d

10

1. b
2. d
3. a
4. a
5. **a.** E; **b.** C; **c.** C; **d.** C; **e.** C

11

1. d
2. a
3. C
4. E
5. b
6. **a.** C; **b.** E

12

1. c
2. E
3. E
4. E
5. C
6. **a.** C; **b.** E; **c.** C
7. C
8. a
9. C

13

1. C
2. a
3. d
4. b
5. b
6. e
7. C
8. a

14

1. d
2. a
3. b
4. e
5. a

15

1. a
2. d
3. a
4. b
5. c
6. E
7. e

Este livro foi composto nas fontes Fedra Sans e Fedra Serif e impresso em maio de 2011 pela Yangraf Gráfica e Editora Ltda, sobre papel offset 90g/m².